ALL MONSTERS MUST DIE

ALL MONSTERS MUST DIE

An Excursion to North Korea

MAGNUS BÄRTÅS & FREDRIK EKMAN

TRANSLATED FROM SWEDISH BY SASKIA VOGEL

ANANSI
INTERNATIONAL

First published by Albert Bonniers Förlag, Stockholm, Sweden
Published in the English language by arrangement with Bonnier Rights, Stockhom,
Sweden, through the Kontext Agency, Stockholm, Sweden

This edition published in 2015 by
House of Anansi Press Inc.
www.houseofanansi.com

House of Anansi Press is committed to protecting our natural environment.
As part of our efforts, the interior of this book is printed on paper that contains
100% post-consumer recycled fibres, is acid-free, and is processed chlorine-free.

20 19 18 17 16   2 3 4 5 6

Library and Archives Canada Cataloguing in Publication

Bärtås, Magnus
[Alla monster måste dö. English]
All monsters must die : an excursion to North Korea / by Magnus
Bärtås and Fredrik Ekman ; translated by Saskia Vogel.

Translation of: Alla monster måste dö.
Includes bibliographical references and index.
Issued in print and electronic formats.
ISBN 978-1-77089-880-6 (pbk.). — ISBN 978-1-77089-881-3 (html)

1. Korea (North) — History. 2. Korea (North) — Social conditions.
3. Korea (North) — Description and travel. 4. Bärtås, Magnus — Travel —
Korea (North). 5. Ekman, Fredrik — Travel — Korea (North).
I. Ekman, Fredrik, author II. Vogel, Saskia, translator III. Title.
IV. Title: Alla monster måste dö. English.

DS935.B3713 2015   951.93   C2015-900796-8
                                                                C2015-900797-6

Library of Congress Control Number: 2016933257

Book design: Alysia Shewchuk

The cost of this translation was defrayed by a subsidy from the Swedish Arts
Council, gratefully acknowledged.

*We acknowledge for their financial support of our publishing program the Canada
Council for the Arts, the Ontario Arts Council, and the Government of Canada through
the Canada Book Fund.*

Printed and bound in Canada

CONTENTS

CHINA

RUSSIA

Punggye-ri
Nuclear Test Site

Mount Baekdu

Samjiyon

Chongjin

Mount Chilbo

Orang

NORTH
KOREA

EAST SEA
(SEA OF JAPAN)

YELLOW
SEA

Pyongyang

D-M-Z

Kaesong

SOUTH
KOREA

38th Parallel

Seoul

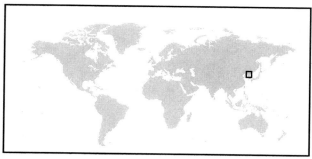

"Everything starts from the individual — the body's pleasures and pains. If you don't see that, you misunderstand history."

— Mourid Barghouti

"'In all my days!' the emperor said. 'A nightingale? I've never heard of such a thing! Is there such a bird in my empire — in my own garden? I want it to come here and sing for me.'"

— "The Nightingale," Hans Christian Andersen

PROLOGUE

1978

IT WAS A mid-January afternoon in Hong Kong. The South Korean actress Choi Eun-hee was strolling along the boardwalk at Repulse Bay, an exclusive resort area dominated by a long beach of golden sand in the southern part of Hong Kong Island. The area attracted wealthy investors — businessmen from around the world who wanted to be part of Hong Kong's explosive expansion. The film industry was blossoming with Cantonese action movies, and Hong Kong had entered the age of television. Recently, two young boys had flung themselves from the seventh storey of a skyscraper in Kowloon City after watching *Ultraman,* a Japanese superhero series. They were convinced that they would glide above the cityscape, just like Ultraman in his red and silver costume.

Choi Eun-hee, or Madame Choi as she was called, was a legend in South Korea. Throughout her acting career she had moved effortlessly between roles: a virtuous housewife, a fair princess, a resolute lawyer, a prostitute living in the barracks of an American military base. As one of the first female directors in South Korean cinema, she was a pioneer. Inspired by Hollywood's studio system, she and her then husband, the director Shin Sang-ok, founded and established a film company. Shin Films produced everything from melodramas, costume dramas, horror, war movies, and musicals to "Wild East" films—the so-called "Manchurian Westerns." In its heyday, the company employed 300 people, and had workshops, prop storage facilities, a printing house, and its own movie theatres.

Choi Eun-hee was on her way to a business meeting with a certain Mr. Wang of Hong Kong Kumjang Film. They were going to discuss various film projects, and Mr. Wang had also pledged financial support to the South Korean film school where Madame Choi was the principal.

THE PRESIDENT OF South Korea at the time was General Park Chung-hee. Having come to power in 1961 after a military *coup d'état* supported by the United States, Park had appointed himself president for life. He quickly established himself as a brutal and thick-skinned leader. In 1974, a man with North Korean sympathies attempted to assassinate the dictator while he was delivering a speech. The man fired a number of rounds before he was overpowered. The bullets missed Park, but one of them hit his wife, who was carried off stage, dying. General Park calmly continued his speech after the worst of the tumult had passed.

Park's callousness and severity were renowned but he also had a soft spot for melodrama. The same year he came to power, Shin and Madame's film *Evergreen Tree (Sangnoksu)* was released in South Korea. Park was moved to tears by the film, calling it a national cinematic epic. Years later, in 1969, General Park was so eager to see the results of a costume drama that Shin Films was shooting that he ordered that the freshly developed negatives be driven straight to the Blue House, the presidential palace in Seoul. For a short period of time, the filmmaking couple were guests of the palace. Shin played cards with the dictator.

NOW, IN 1978, everything had changed. The days of card games in the presidential palace in Seoul were a distant memory for Madame Choi. General Park was at the height of his autocratic power, and South Korean society had become subject to extreme authoritarian rule. No criticisms of the government could be uttered. A construction worker in Seoul had just been sentenced to six months in prison for claiming that the largest pumpkins on the peninsula could be found in North Korea. He was convicted of having praised the enemy power. While on trial he stood his ground, saying: "Everyone knows it's true that—" He was interrupted by the judge, who told him: "Your crime is that you've said this in a public place."

The same fate could befall those who collected Soviet stamps, which could be considered an indication of Communist sympathies. Men of the cloth and intellectuals were placed under house arrest for the slightest suggestion of protest against the regime; long-haired students were captured on the streets and dragged to police stations for compulsory haircuts. As if by reflex, the police charged at every gathering that hinted at opposition. When a group of students assembled in central Seoul to hand out flyers, a large posse of police arrived on the scene and immediately let their nightsticks wail. The police didn't notice that the flyers were just blank pages.

MADAME CHOI HAD had a hard time arranging the meeting with Mr. Wang, and she couldn't understand why. He'd started off so insistent, sending her a script that he wanted her to direct, letting her know about upcoming parts in Hong Kong films, and courting her in person at the film school. Madame was flattered, but a touch concerned. She was fifty-one years old and under no illusions: her glory days were gone. Hong Kong had plenty of young, promising directors. Why did Mr. Wang want her, specifically? The film school didn't make money, but cost all the more. She had been playing parts in South Korean television dramas, but still times were tough. She had to take what came her way.

This was the first time that Madame had ever travelled outside of Korea. While she'd been waiting to hear from Mr. Wang, Kim Guh-wha, an employee at the Shin Films office in Hong Kong, had taken pity on her and introduced her to an acquaintance, Lee Sang-hee, also a Korean. Together they killed time shopping, lunching, and going on excursions, always accompanied by Lee's seven-year-old daughter.

4

Madame was with Lee and her daughter, strolling along, unhurried, past the glamorous Repulse Bay Hotel. Built in 1920 in the British colonial style, the storied hotel had been made famous by the Hollywood classic *Love Is a Many-Splendored Thing*. But after ten days in Hong Kong, Madame was tired of being a tourist and tired of waiting; she wanted to get back to the film school. She couldn't drink in the pleasures of the afternoon. Only the odd person came walking along the shore. It was not a cold winter, but the people of Hong Kong were wrapped up in layers.

Sailboats and motorboats were tied to the docks that jutted out from the sandy beach. When they passed one of these moorings, some of Lee's friends called out to them. The men offered to give them a ride to the Kumjang Film offices, and that way they'd save some time. Madame assumed the men were Hong Kong Chinese. She noted their long, groomed hair—a hairstyle that hip Hong Kong Chinese people wore. They climbed aboard, but once the boat left the dock it sailed straight out into the open sea. Madame began to worry. She turned to Lee and asked what was going on. Lee didn't answer. Instead, she calmly took out a cigarette and lit it; then she took one out for Madame and handed it to her.

One of the men approached Madame and in shaky Korean explained that he was also a "Joseon-person," meaning that he too was of Korean descent.

"Where are we going?" asked Madame.

"Into General Kim Il-sung's great embrace," the man responded.

It was in that moment that she finally understood what

was happening. Her heart pounded, the blood drained from her head, and she fainted.

WHEN MADAME CAME to, her arms were bound to her body and she was being transported onto a larger boat, a cargo ship, where she was put in the captain's quarters. Madame shouted that she had a family to take care of, and she banged her head against the wall until they stuck a needle in her arm. When she woke up, they were on the open sea, the boat careening through the waves. She heard Lee's screams and cries coming from somewhere on the boat. Lee had led Madame straight into the trap, but she hadn't counted on being taken away with her daughter.

AFTER EIGHT DAYS at sea, they arrived at the North Korean harbour town of Nampo. Madame hesitantly climbed the stairs to the quay and looked around. Two functionaries in scarves and overcoats were waiting for her. One smiled courteously, and then a photographer snapped a picture that she would carry with her. She was wearing black sunglasses and a trench coat with the collar turned up. One hand was over her mouth, while the other was holding the coat closed at her chest. It was January 22, 1978, at four o'clock in the afternoon, a cold day.

A black limousine was parked on the quay. The back door opened and a short man with an unusual hairstyle and a child-like face stepped out. He smiled expectantly and said: "Thank you for coming, Madame Choi. I'm Kim Jong-il."

THE SHORT MAN was President Kim Il-sung's son, who was the head of the Propaganda and Agitation Department in North Korea. By this time, Kim Jong-il had held many posts within the Communist Party's Central Committee and was already called "Dear Leader" and "Wise Leader." There was no doubt that he was the favourite son.

Madame Choi was invited to take a seat in the back of his limousine. En route to Pyongyang, he gave her a spontaneous tour, pointing out places of interest. The minister of propaganda was as happy as a hero taking her around the capital, where his father's giant portrait adorned many buildings. Then they headed out to the countryside, where the villages were bleak. After passing fruit groves and a shooting range, they arrived at one of Kim Jong-il's private residences, a luxurious mansion surrounded by a tall fence. Madame Choi was asked to hand over her passport and ID card.

*　*　*

ON HER FIRST morning in North Korea, Choi Eun-hee woke up to flowers from Kim Jong-il. A doctor, the same person who had given her the shot on the cargo ship, came to check on her health. He gave her vitamin injections.

She was dressed and photographed in a *hanbok*, the traditional folk dress. *Hanbok* is the Korean equivalent of the kimono, but less refined and also often made of richly coloured fabric. A *hanbok* obscures the female form, making the woman wearing it radiate virtuousness. Kim Jong-il made sure the photos were sent to his father, who replied that Madame's beauty was still intact and the *joseonot*—the North Korean word for *hanbok*—suited her well.

Choi Eun-hee didn't know why she had been taken to North Korea, and Kim Jong-il offered no explanation. After six days he arranged a welcome dinner. The minister of propaganda was in high spirits and talked endlessly. When he addressed his subordinates, they jumped up mid-chew, as if their chairs had given them a shock.

"Well, Madame Choi, what do you think of my appearance?" he asked. "I'm a small, tubby dwarf, correct?"

He laughed, and everyone else dared to join in with the laughter. Even Madame Choi couldn't help but laugh.

After that, she didn't see much of him.

MEANWHILE, MADAME'S EX-HUSBAND, the director Shin Sang-ok, was trying to establish a name for himself in the United States after his life's work had been demolished by General Park Chung-hee. It was while living in America that he found out Madame Choi had vanished without a trace during a trip to Hong Kong. He contacted Kim Hong-wook, a former South Korean CIA chief, to help with the search for his ex-wife. Like so many others, Kim was living in exile after having fallen out of favour with General Park. After filing for permanent residency in the United States, Shin left for Hong Kong.

In South Korea, the media and the police were in agreement that the director was behind the disappearance of Madame, and when Shin arrived in Hong Kong the South Korean authorities were immediately on his trail. Then, just six months after Choi Eun-hee's disappearance, events repeated themselves: under the pretense of a meeting with potential financiers, Shin was kidnapped by Kim Jong-il's agents in Hong Kong and put on a boat to North Korea.

The year was 1978, the thirtieth anniversary of the founding of the Democratic People's Republic of Korea.

TO PYONGYANG

SEPTEMBER 2008. Thirty years have passed since Choi Eun-hee and Shin Sang-ok were kidnapped, and sixty years since North Korea became a nation. We have taken our seats on the plane at Beijing Capital International Airport, en route to Pyongyang. Small screens fold down from the ceiling. An air hostess wearing a ruby-red uniform appears on the screens, multiplies. She welcomes us aboard this Air Koryo flight, bows, and says the journey will be run on Juche-power. Then she thanks "the Great Leader Kim Il-sung" and smiles broadly.

We look down at the magazine that has been handed out instead of the usual duty-free shopping catalogue. The cover shows a large, futuristic city in soft pastel colours — there are pistachio and pink façades, light ochre- and umber-coloured skyscrapers. Pyongyang. Here greenery is shown among the houses; there is a river and a perfect bridge. In the foreground, three smiling generations of North Koreans are looking up and beyond the border of the frame.

The magazine was published in the year 97. We are on our way to a parallel universe with a different calendar.

INSIDE THE MAGAZINE we are served up an image of the world that is totally divorced from the one we are accustomed to. Here are reports on North Korea's successful goat farmers, recently completed cinemas, idyllic villages. Public healthcare has led to seventy- and eighty-year-old North Korean men running marathons and performing onstage. All thanks to the leader Kim Jong-il, and not least for the miraculous mineral water from Ryongkasan, which is superior to all other mineral water found around the world and even cures catarrh of the colon.

In an article on the fishing industry there are pictures of a trawler and wooden boats where the nets are pulled up by hand. In one picture of a harbour, there are four trucks in an almost too-perfect row. When you look more closely you see that it's the same polished truck, multiplied.

It's not all peachy in the magazine. One piece of reportage discusses long-range missiles, submarines armed with atomic weapons, and tens of thousands of South Korean and American soldiers who have mobilized in the South under the pretense of military exercises. These drills are in fact practice for a future attack on North Korea.

THE LANDING STRIP at Pyongyang Sunan International Airport is enormous. The terminal isn't as grand. Once we get inside, a VIP lane is immediately created for the Cuban ambassador and his wife. When we leave the terminal we see a pair of black Mercedes together with a welcoming committee holding flower arrangements for the Cuban emissary.

Being part of an organized tourist trip is the only way for us to get into North Korea. You can't travel on your own, and you can't be a journalist or an author — but you can be an artist. Our previous books, we had explained during the visa process in Stockholm, are exclusively about art, and the functionaries at the North Korean embassy were satisfied with this. And so we were granted permission to take an eight-day grand tour of Pyongyang and the countryside. The schedule is packed: Panmunjom, Kaesong, Baekdu Mountain, and other places of which we have only vague notions.

We form a crowd of pale Westerners — we are all young or middle-aged men with the exception of Oksana, a Ukrainian woman with a long ponytail who lives and works in South Korea. Our cell phones are confiscated by a guide, who puts them all in a plastic bag that is taped tightly until it becomes a big plastic cocoon. Our passports are also collected.

The chartered bus sets out on the wide, tree-lined avenues toward Pyongyang. On board is the group of people with whom we'll be forced to spend the next eight days, from early in the morning to late at night. Our every step will be monitored and we'll be herded back together as soon as anyone ventures a few steps in the wrong direction or lags behind. There are twenty-two of us, including two young Swedish farmers from Värmland, a district in the western countryside; three even younger men from the posh Stockholm suburb of Bromma, wearing brightly coloured polo shirts; a very large and well-built Swiss man called Bruno; a Swedish fighter pilot, who strangely enough was given a visa in spite of his military post; a happy, bald Norwegian named Trond; a tattooed baker of Czech heritage; Andrei, a wiry Russian chemist; a Gothenburger called Nils who lives in Minsk; a Ukrainian wearing camouflage pants who is Oksana's colleague in South Korea; and Ari, a Dutch KLM employee. Elias, who is the youngest in the group, sat next to us on the plane. He was immersed in maps and took frantic notes. We thought he was writing in code, but when he saw us looking at his notebook he explained that he isn't used to writing by hand — he grew up with computers. North Korea has been a consuming interest for him since he was thirteen. Now he's barely twenty and this is the journey of his life. His eyes shine when he sees the rice paddies glinting beyond the avenues.

The guides introduce themselves as Mr. Song and Ms. Kim. Ms. Kim speaks Russian when addressing the chemist, the only one in the group who doesn't understand English and who is taking his first-ever trip abroad. Ms. Kim is twenty-one but she could just as well be fourteen, going by her looks. She wears a pink dress with slightly padded shoulders. Mr. Song, a small man with a centre parting and gummy smile, and wearing a short-sleeved white shirt and suit pants, is just a few years older than Ms. Kim. He is in charge.

He begins by listing a number of simple housekeeping rules: we are never allowed to leave the group of our own volition; we are not allowed to take pictures without asking; we should show respect to the people we meet; we should also show respect to photographs of Kim Il-sung, the departed father of Kim Jong-il. We are absolutely not allowed to fold the airplane magazine, sit on it, or throw it away because it contains Kim Il-sung's portrait. On second thought, it's probably best that he collects the magazines before any accidents happen.

North Korea can be called the world's only necrocracy— a country that is officially run by a deceased person. In July 1994, when a tearful news anchor announced Kim Il-sung's death on North Korean state television, mass hysteria broke out. We have seen the official mourning video on YouTube: there is crying in the schools, in the factories, at parades, and at home. Veterans in wheelchairs bawl and people in crowds hit themselves with their fists until they fall to the ground. Like a film within a film, those at home are shown casting themselves at their televisions in despair as his funeral is broadcast. These are violent scenes in which small children are crying, probably out of fear of the adults' behaviour.

No one knew how to fill the hole the leader left behind. For four years, the presidential post was left unoccupied. Then, in 1998, the position of president was written out of the constitution. Kim Il-sung was named Eternal President of the Democratic People's Republic of Korea. The previous year, Kim Jong-il had been given the more modest title of General Secretary of the Workers' Party of Korea, even though he was already acting as the new dictator.

AFTER TRAVELLING THE long, orderly avenues, we enter the capital. We are driven along huge boulevards with few cars. The flat topography makes it seem like all the buildings are rising from one and the same plane. There is much greenery, large open parks, enormous monuments, boxy apartment complexes in glazed tile, and everywhere there are mosaics of Kim Il-sung. Homes, façades, and streets are worn but clean. The ground-floor windows of all residential buildings are equipped with thick metal bars.

The lack of traffic makes it seem like the city has been taken over by pedestrians. People criss-cross the giant streets, and buses honk incessantly at jaywalkers and the occasional cyclist. We come to understand that honking is part of driving here. Even our bus driver honks as soon as anyone appears on the road.

To our surprise, we see a large commercial billboard. It features an ad for the Hwiparam ("Whistle") model from the domestic car manufacturer Pyeonghwa. Modelled on the Fiat Siena, named by Kim Jong-il, financed by the South Korean cult leader Moon Sun-myung, and manufactured in North Korea, the car is a remarkable, political-composite product — "a strong and beautiful car," as it says in the ad. The factory produces a few hundred cars a year, and each vehicle is sold for a price that's beyond the means of even wealthy North Koreans. The billboard is the first sign we see of the unholy alliance between Kim Jong-il and the super-rich Pastor Moon, best known for officiating mass wedding ceremonies between his cult followers.

We come to a halt at a crossing and have a chance to

observe a young, female traffic officer, placed like a living sculpture in the middle of the intersection. She wears a chalk-white uniform jacket, a blue skirt, and white ankle socks. She stands at attention, with a short stick in her hand, never moving from her spot. Then she quickly looks left and right, her right arm shoots up, and she turns her body ninety degrees. Frozen in this new position, she takes a nearly imperceptible sidestep with her left foot, then gives instructions to a car that she's registered with an incredibly quick glance over her shoulder. The car passes and the woman swiftly lowers her stick while simultaneously making a half turn, straight as a nail around her own axle like a figurine in a music box. It is as if she wants to emphasize the movement of the passing cars.

The few traffic lights we see are shut off. There seems to be a lack of electricity to power them. These traffic lights use five colours, probably the only place in the world that does.

The bus drives us right into the heart of Pyongyang, to the Victorious Fatherland Liberation War Museum on Kim Il-sung Square, a giant building made of marble and granite. We are led into the damp, cool, hangar-like cellar where the strict, uniformed female guide presents trophies of war: helmets, uniforms, weapons, shot-down war planes, a plane that is said to have carried biological weapons, a helicopter, as well as a model of the USS *Pueblo*, a seized American spy ship. Each time we leave a room, the lights are turned off behind us. In the middle of the tour there's a power outage. The guide doesn't acknowledge it; she resolutely continues, and in the dark we clumsily orient ourselves to the banging of her heels.

On the top floor, there is a slowly rotating viewing deck where we sit in front of a cyclorama depicting the 1950 Battle of Daejeon, which North Korean history has deemed the turning point in the Korean War. Forty artists have painted a backdrop to the display of barbed wire, bunkers, and real tanks and jeeps. It's an astounding, illusory scene depicting a plethora of action. Some of the props are actual relics from the war, the guide says. She also says that one million people are represented on the canvas, which measures 103 metres in length by 58 metres in height. We all conclude from just a few glances that this, of course, is impossible.

The guide doesn't mention the reports that came out just before our arrival in Pyongyang. In South Korea, it's been said that North Korean soldiers massacred civilians after their victory at the Battle of Daejeon. But photographs bearing "confidential" stamps and documents from the American army's archives, which had just been released in July 2008, show that it was the South Korean troops who carried out the massacre before they retreated. Between 3,000 and 7,000 civilian men and women suspected of having Communist sympathies were killed, along with their children, and the American command was aware of the whole thing. Maybe the news hasn't reached our guide; maybe these atrocities have long been known here. Even though the events illustrate the South's ruthless war crimes, she doesn't draw attention to them.

The British journalist Alan Winnington, who followed

North Korean troops during the Korean War, saw the hastily dug mass graves where hands and feet stuck out from the earth. He wrote about the events in the British Communist newspaper the *Daily Worker*, but was accused of lying by the American embassy in London. And the U.S. military advisor Frank Winslow recently testified that the American command was invited by the South Koreans to witness the "turkey shoot" — the name given to the mass executions carried out next to the ditches that served as graves. Winslow declined, but other officers went. A few of them photographed the events.

In one of the pictures from the newly opened archive, a still-living teenage boy is about to tumble into a mass grave. The bodies form a grotesque jumble of arms, heads, and legs. The boy is lying on his stomach, while a soldier holds on to his bare feet. He is tied to his murdered comrade; they lie side by side. The corpse's arm is stretched across the boy's back as though he is seeking warmth in his sleep. They're about to accompany each other to the grave. The photographer has caught the eye of the still-living boy. His head hangs over the edge of the grave, but his face is turned and he looks straight into the camera.

In 2005, the South Korean government formed the Truth and Reconciliation Commission, which is excavating Daejeon. It is thought that more than 100,000 Communist sympathizers were executed after war broke out in 1950. And Daejeon is just one of many places where massacres were carried out: 1,800 were killed in Suwon, 10,000 in Pusan, 25,000 in the southern part of Gyeongsang Province. In each of these places, remnants of bone are still being discovered in the soil.

* * *

THE BUS TAKES us to the Yanggakdo Hotel, where we are sequestered from the rest of the city. The forty-seven-storey building is situated on an island in the Taedong River, which runs through Pyongyang, dividing the city east and west. We're not allowed to leave the island unaccompanied. There's a greenhouse for growing vegetables, a golf course, and a movie theatre.

As one of the few places in North Korea where foreigners are permitted, the Yanggakdo Hotel has a mythic aura. Here, sharks from the black market mix with diplomats, businessmen, shock tourists and regular tourists, various politicians, and envoys from marginal leftist groups. The Yanggakdo Hotel plays a leading role in Canadian illustrator Guy Delisle's 2005 graphic novel *Pyongyang: A Journey in North Korea*. Delisle lived here for a two-month period and in his book he describes the rituals of this strange place that incubates secrets and hidden rooms. Like all foreigners, Delisle's freedom of movement in Pyongyang was strictly limited, and so he spent many long hours in the Yanggakdo Hotel. He had found himself at the hotel after a film project he was involved with as an animator ran out of money. It's not unusual that foreign animation projects at the edge of ruin end up in Pyongyang; here, you have the chance to finish them at a low cost. SEK Studio in central Pyongyang, where Delisle worked, is one of the world's largest animation studios, with 1,600 employees. Animation is one of North Korea's few successful industries—perhaps the only one after the manufacturing of weapons. *Pororo the Little Penguin*, a hugely popular South Korean series, is made here. Kim Jong-il is said to have personally given this show his blessing. He had long advocated on behalf of the production of animated series. There is said to be a motivational plaque outside of the Ministry of Culture in Pyongyang that reads: "make more animated films."

AT FIRST GLANCE, everything in the Yanggakdo Hotel is as it is in Delisle's graphic novel: the giant sea turtle lying as if in a coma within the small, sparse aquarium just inside the entrance; the gift shop behind the elevators with its limited selection, and next to it the pictures of Kim Jong-il who, according to the plaque beneath, provides "on-the-spot guidance" around the country; the restaurants on the ground floor, which are still called Restaurant No. 1, Restaurant No. 2, and Restaurant No. 3.

One difference is the jostling crowd in the spacious lobby; the hotel was more desolate when Delisle spent time here. The collected mass is connected to North Korea's sixtieth anniversary celebrations. The games, the parades, and all the other manifestations of celebration will be more intensive than usual.

Erik Cornell, Sweden's first chargé d'affaires in Pyongyang, mentions in his book *North Korea under Communism: Report of an Envoy to Paradise* that in the 1970s, just thirteen or fourteen Western adults were living in Pyongyang. Today, that group amounts to about one hundred residents. Since Cornell published his book, tourism has increased. A few thousand Western tourists visit North Korea every year, whereas around 7 million tourists will visit South Korea this year.

It's hard to say how many Chinese, Japanese, and South Koreans visit the country. During the few years of détente between South and North Korea (from approximately 2002 to 2008), South Korean visitors flooded into special, enclosed tourist areas. But in the past years the influx has been stemmed. Average North Koreans, of course, don't have the option of leaving the country.

THE HOTEL ROOM looks like any other hotel room. We find ourselves high up in the building. We pull back the curtains and open the window. The sun is setting, dyeing the sky yellow. The smoke from the chimneys of the distant factories forms a veil with a red, glowing fringe where it meets the sun. As night falls, the skyscrapers on the other side of the river turn blue.

After unpacking we run into Elias, the North Korea enthusiast, in the elevator. He is bursting with curiosity and wants to investigate everything: the hotel, the city, and the people who live here. He has already managed to wander around the island, but when he reached the bridge leading off it he was immediately stopped. Now he's riding the elevator, trying to gain access to each floor. On some, he's sent away.

In the dining room, we get to talking with an American who married into a Japanese brewing family. He has a generic appearance and a perfect East Coast smile, like a model in a Gant ad. As an American, he's allowed to stay in North Korea for just four days. So he can't join us on the tour around the country, and has to stick to the sights in Pyongyang. He tells us about the North Korean beer Taedong, which takes its name from the mighty river that runs through Pyongyang. It tastes like a real British ale should—and for good reason. In 2000, Kim Jong-il bought an entire brewery in Trowbridge, England. As soon as the British owner was provided with a guarantee that the brewery wouldn't be used to create biological weapons, the sale was completed. The brewery was dismantled, shipped to North Korea, and put back together. Since then, the supply of beer in North Korea has been secured.

The North Korean Taepodong missiles are often mistakenly called "Taedong missiles." Beer bottles and missiles, the shapes are indeed similar. In an ad on Korean Central Television (KCTV)—the North Korean state television—a tasting is conducted by laboratory personnel. The bottles float around in space and columns of foam shoot up like missiles.

After a few Taedongs, the American confides in us about his life in Japan. His stepfather has fully accepted him—he's next in line to take over the brewery—but there's one problem.

"Here's the truth," he says. "I don't have a single Japanese friend." He swallows a sip of beer with a quick grimace and looks around. He realizes the room has fallen silent. He quickly reinstates his smile and suggests that we continue talking in the panorama bar.

When we reach the circular restaurant, which is on the forty-seventh floor of the hotel, the American immediately starts flirting with the waitresses. They smile indulgently. The restaurant is supposed to rotate, but you don't notice. Someone places a coin on the floor and, yes, after a while we can see that the coin is farther away.

Twilight has fallen quickly. Now it's pitch dark. When we look out the window, we don't see a panoramic view. The lights across town are shut off, and the odd single point of light doesn't give the impression that Pyongyang is a big city. It is unknown how many people actually live here, but soon there'll be a census. At last count, there were 2.7 million inhabitants.

CAN YOU IMAGINE?

THE WINDOWS IN our hotel room are wide open. We turned off the air conditioner overnight and let the humidity flood in. Pyongyang is cloaked in a dense fog. We can hear voices on loudspeakers in the distance. We stand by the windows, and after a while we start to make out indeterminate movements on the boulevard on the other side of the Taedong River. Details become discernible: we see hundreds of tanks slowly moving forward in a line like a parade of woodlice, while a stream of people, many holding red flags, heads in the opposite direction. The people hurry along, the voices on the loudspeakers urging them on between interludes of revolutionary music.

WE EAT BREAKFAST in Restaurant No. 1. Two omelette chefs crowned with exaggeratedly tall toques have their own table at the far end of the room. Deeply focused, they beat the eggs with slim wooden spoons. There's also a buffet displaying everything from continental breakfast to kimchi. The graphic novelist Guy Delisle had plenty of time to ponder at breakfast. He concluded that the toothpicks on the table must have been hand-carved. We don't see any of these toothpicks, but we do enjoy the omelettes. They are outstanding.

The American turns up, but avoids making eye contact. He sits at another table.

THE BUS TAKES us through the city, where masses of people are performing tasks early this Sunday morning. One woman squats down and scrubs the cobblestones on a traffic island with a root brush and water. Other people are plucking something from the grass-covered viaducts. Members of the Korean Youth Corps wear red kerchiefs and walk in a row, and other groups move in unison too. Every other person seems to be wearing a uniform, and not only the brown Home Guard uniform. In addition to the police, the military police, and the traffic police, even those who maintain the roads wear uniforms.

The roads are wide but there are few bicycles and cars. We notice that some of the cars are Volvo 144s. They have driven here for nearly forty years. They were shipped from Sweden in 1973 together with drilling equipment from Atlas Copco. The North Koreans didn't bother paying the $503,743,731 bill for the drills, the 600 cars, and a number of other things. The Swedish Export Credit Corporation hasn't given up hope yet; they've come up with a payment plan. If they make their half-yearly payments, the North Korean government will have paid them back by 2019. But why should North Korea repay the money to Sweden? They've had gigantic debts since the start of the 1970s, when they frantically bought goods from Europe and Japan. When foreign businessmen and diplomats asked when these bills would be paid, they were met with blank looks: shouldn't the rest of the world be grateful to do business with North Korea?

WE PASS A pyramid-like structure in the distance and are amazed at its enormous size. At 371 metres tall, with 101 floors above ground and 4 below, the Ryugyong Hotel is only ten metres shorter than the Empire State Building. Construction began in 1987 and was halted in 1992. Since then the building has been abandoned, like an epic monument to failure. Our guide Mr. Song says its slogan was: "If a newborn checks into the hotel with the intention of spending one night in each room, that person will be twenty-seven years old by the time they check out." On second thought, this seems like an unlikely slogan.

Mr. Song also tells us that an Egyptian telephone company has invested money in the hotel, and it is hoped that renovations will be completed by the centenary of Kim Il-sung's birth in 2012.[*] In the past, Ryugyong Hotel was often Photoshopped out of official pictures of Pyongyang, but

---

* In November 2012, the hotel was taken over by the Germany luxury hotel chain Kempinski, which announced that in 2013 the renovations would be completed and the hotel would be ready to be inaugurated. But in March 2013, Kempinski's now-retired president and CEO, Reto Wittwer, stated that the firm had pulled out of the project.

the authorities have since decided that it does indeed exist, and we can attest to the fact that the building's sheer size asserts its existence with tectonic force. The North Korean press has already started setting the tone for the reopening, calling the hotel "a phoenix ceaselessly reaching for the sky."

At once massive and ethereal, the hotel rises up and towers over all the other buildings. It inspires fantasies, new terms, and virtual representations around the world. The Italian architect Stefano Boeri once said that the design had "forced it to reveal its icy nature, its irresistible fascination as a fragile alien meteorite." Ryugyong Hotel is, according to Boeri, "the only built piece of science fiction in the contemporary world." Other epithets are just as fantastic: the "white elephant," the "Hotel of Doom," the "ghost hotel," and the "Death Star."

THE BUS DRIVES us back to the airport. It's a bit disappointing to be leaving Pyongyang so soon after we've arrived, but according to the itinerary we're supposed to fly to Chongjin in North Hamgyong Province to experience the coastal landscape near the Russian border.

The airport is completely deserted. The arrival and departure screens don't display any destinations; they are blank. Apparently, we're the only people flying out of Pyongyang today. Average North Koreans aren't allowed to travel domestically without special dispensation. And if they are given permission, then their mode of transport is a bus or train. That's why there are no regularly scheduled domestic flights in the country.

A fog hangs over the airport. The Air Koryo planes are lined up in a row on the endless runway that disappears into the haze. A Russian Antonov from the 1950s has taxied out: this is our plane.

Climbing the stairs into the aircraft, most of us look like regular tourists, wearing T-shirts and shorts and holding cameras. Bruno, the Swiss man, is as big as a house. When he speaks, he sounds like Arnold Schwarzenegger. But his isn't a gym-built body, we imagine; it's an Alpine body shaped by butter, fresh air, and mountain treks. The blond Swedish fighter pilot follows Bruno. At almost six feet, five inches tall, he towers over the rest of us. But compared to Bruno, he looks small.

Ari, the young Dutch KLM employee with a flat cap and a drowsy look, has a more sophisticated camera than the rest of us. He uses different lenses and is always looking for fresh angles. It was clear from the moment we landed that this group trip would include an inferno of photography. However, Mr. Song has given us strict instructions: *Photography is only permitted of approved subject matter. Do not photograph people and absolutely do not photograph military personnel. In the countryside you basically can't take a picture of anything.* Still, the group is not discouraged and we are happily taking pictures of each other. As we climb aboard, flashbulbs pop as if we were on the red carpet.

* * *

THROUGH THE WINDOW of the plane, the North Korean landscape seems frighteningly inaccessible: barren, rippling mountains the colour of granite; clusters of brown barracks forming villages and compounds. Other images are burned in the mind's eye—satellite pictures, scenes from Google Earth, photographs from the Cold War of parachuting spies landing on the ground, never to return. The aircraft's windshield is like a monitor. The sound of the propellers intensifies this notion. You could disappear in this landscape.

But when we alight at the military airport in Orang, south of Chongjin, a pleasant, balmy wind is coursing gently over the runway. Built by the Imperial Japanese Army, the airbase is hemmed in by green fields that stretch as far as the eye can see. In the distance, we see people following paths over the terrain.

Sacks of rice and crates of beer are carried from the plane. Two small buses await us; the drivers are in the process of swabbing up fish waste in one of them. As soon as we have disembarked, Elias bends down and presses his hand to the ground. He then whips out his notebook, jots something down, and moves restlessly about on the runway.

Mr. Song is watching him with a troubled gaze. Elias doesn't know which way to turn. Everything—every bush and every person—is interesting. Everything demands his attention at once. We understand. What we're seeing has been a restricted zone for so long that the country is like a social biosphere with its own conditions for life. The idea of North Korea as a living laboratory—especially when compared to South Korea, its "twin," separated at birth—is shared by many political researchers, economists, and sociologists. But it has been impossible to conduct any studies here.

THE NEAREST CITY, Chongjin, is Shin Sang-ok's birthplace. Madame's husband, the famous film director, grew up here in the 1930s, when there wasn't a North or a South Korea. From 1910 until 1945, Korea was a Japanese colony. It was an unrelenting occupation, in which every tactic was used to Japanify the country.

Shin travelled to Tokyo when he was a teenager to attend art school. The country was first divided after the Second World War. He was nineteen when the Japanese were forced to leave Korea. He then returned to the South to work as a scenographer on Choi In-kyu's *Long Live Freedom*, the first Korean film made after independence. During the occupation Choi had made films that celebrated the colonial power, but the first film he made once the oppressors retreated was an epic about the resistance movement.

Chongjin today is a stricken place. What was once a small fishing village became an industrial port city during the Japanese occupation, when a giant steelworks was erected in the area. Since the fall of the Soviet Union, the factories have been in poor condition and are poisoning the city air. Some of the buildings have been abandoned and are no more than giant, dilapidated monuments of rust. In 1997 Tun Myat, one of the first senior UN officials to visit Chongjin, described the place as a "forest of scrap metal," unique in its decay.

From 1995 to 1998, Chongjin was hit hard by the country's great famine. During the "Arduous March," as the catastrophe was dubbed by officials, the region suffered one of the highest death tolls in the country. In *Nothing to Envy*, author Barbara Demick states that the population in Chongjin—which in the 1970s was North Korea's second-biggest city after Pyongyang—had nearly halved after the famine. This drop in the region's population was not only the result of severe malnourishment, but also of an organized relocation of residents to other areas of the country.

WE LEAVE THE airport through an archway that bears a sign saying: LET US FIGHT TO THE DEATH FOR KIM JONG-IL. Outside we see two gaunt boys squatting at the side of the road. They're picking something out of the grass and putting it into plastic bags.

The fish smell has seeped into the floor of the bus. The odour ripens in the warmth and will linger for hours. Along the dusty gravel roads, people are sweeping, creating small swirls of yellow clouds that are illuminated by the sun. We pass rice paddies and salt pools right next to the sea. Large letters spelling out a Kim Il-sung quote (KOREA IS THE BEST COUNTRY) and a nationalistic invocation (PROCEED JOYFULLY IN SPITE OF HARDSHIP) have been placed in the fields.

It's going to be a long trip on this bumpy road. Oksana, the Ukrainian woman, talks uninterrupted for two hours about life at the South Korean company where she works. We nod dutifully, though we'd prefer to take in the landscape. In certain places along the coast, electric fences have

31

been erected on foundations in the water. We see villages in the distance, poor but not destitute. People walk along roads that aren't a far cry from those built in pre-industrial Europe. Even bicycles aren't a given. We pass the odd truck with its bed full of people, the occasional military vehicle, and now and then an ox-drawn cart. Mr. Song says we're not allowed to take pictures of anything here.

Toward the afternoon, as the road starts to climb, we are allowed to take our cameras out. The mountains and the pine forests remind us of Chinese landscape paintings. As we drive on, we see a number of people gathered by a stream in a small ravine. Two women are dancing on a large boulder. It's almost too idyllic. Have they been placed here on this heavily regulated route as a folkloric feature? Or are we being far too wary of falling into the propaganda trap?

In *Illusive Utopia,* the scholar Kim Suk-young recounts the story of a U.S. statesman who was studying Pyongyang's street life from his hotel window. The American realized that the same people kept coming out of the subway station outside his hotel, and he came to the conclusion that they were actors, hired by the state, who somewhere had a costume repository where they traded overcoats, bags, and umbrellas with each other. All in order to convincingly play commuters at a subway station that might even be defunct.

Defectors have spoken of actors who appear on the streets where foreign dignitaries are driven. Military personnel dress up in civilian clothes to play pedestrians, drivers, and shoppers. On these streets, a thousand people can be assembled for a performance. Kim Suk-young describes North Korea as a theatrical nation, "directing its citizens as if they were actors playing stereotypical roles found in revolutionary operas."

This artifice may recall a childhood fantasy that everything around you is an illusion; that the world is one big set-up, carefully engineered each day so that you'll be lulled into believing in the status quo; that all the strangers you meet are instructed not to let on about the set-up, and their nonchalance is an act in the same way that nearby neighbourhoods are no more than impermanent sets. Sometimes you try to expose the trick with a sudden turn of your head, hoping to catch a glimpse of the stagehands at the edge of the set. Sometimes when you go into town you stop on a dime, tear yourself from your parent's hand so you can rush back around the corner in hope of catching out the machinery in motion.

* * *

THE BUS HAS taken us high up in the terrain. We have stopped to admire the notable cliff formations on Mount Chilbo. We are now very close to where a nuclear weapons test was carried out on October 9, 2006 — a fact that no one in the group mentions, if they happen to be aware of it. We are told that very few tourists visit here, only around thirty people per year.

As we take in the untouched, pine-clad mountain, we have a hard time imagining that only tens of miles away, an atom bomb was detonated just two years ago. The underground test was conducted in Punggye-ri Nuclear Test Site, a system of tunnels built beneath a glen outside of Kilju County, in the southern part of North Hamgyong Province. The Korean Central News Agency (KCNA) reported that the action "brought happiness to our military and people" and was "a great leap forward in the building of a great, prosperous, powerful socialist nation." The event sent waves of fear across Asia and around the world.

Two weeks later, U.S. Secretary of State Condoleezza Rice travelled to China, Japan, and South Korea to advocate the complete isolation of North Korea. The United Nations Security Council unanimously adopted Resolution 1718, the strictest international measure against North Korea since the Korean War. The resolution stated that the international community was to block all sales and transfer of material related to North Korea's nuclear capabilities, from missile systems to unconventional weapons programs. Perhaps because the power of the measure wasn't trusted, nor the ability to monitor North Korea's exchange of weapons technology with countries like Iran, Yemen, and Syria, a condition was added that pointed the sharp end of the stick at what was assumed to be Kim Jong-il's weak spot — his consumption of luxury goods. This was the end of the importation of Hennessy Paradis — one of Hennessy's most expensive cognacs — iPods, Fender Stratocasters, snowmobiles, and flat-screen televisions wider than twenty-nine inches. There was also an embargo on cosmetics, perfumes, luxury carpets, tapestries, fine bone china, designer apparel, and gemstones such as diamonds, sapphires, rubies, and emeralds. This list of luxury goods may seem randomly chosen, but it was precise. It is Kim Jong-il's usual shopping list turned into a UN resolution.

A LOCAL GUIDE — a gaunt man with a flat chest and endearing charm — arrives to tell us about the boulders in the landscape before us. His English is far from perfect, but he is intent on making himself understood. He says that he will inform us of the history of the stones, but he doesn't impart any geological or historical data — instead, he tells us nationalist myths.

And the myths aren't even old. They go back only one generation to the fight against the Japanese colonizers. The guide recounts that the boulders depict two people tenderly leaning against each other, representing the brave Korean soldier returning from the war against Japan to a loving reunion with his wife. Indeed, it looks like one of the stones in the formation is clutching the other. The guide gives us a sly look and tells us that the wife has longed so much for her husband that she can't help but reach out her hand. He doesn't say it outright, but he implies that she has a tight grip on his private parts.

"Can you imagine?" he says, smiling and looking at each of us. "Can you imagine?"

A bit farther south, a giant boulder lies horizontally on a number of smaller rocks. The guide tells us that when Kim Jong-il came here, he immediately renamed the formation. It was originally called the Stone Table, but in the dictator's eyes it wasn't a table, it was a piano. Since then, it's been called Piano Rock.

"Can you imagine?" he says again.

No matter how much we try to picture it, we don't see a piano. But because this is the image that sprung up in the leader's head, it will be a piano for all eternity.

ON OUR WAY back down the mountain, we stop at a Buddhist monastery. Mr. Song says that the monks are away, but it's doubtful that any religious activity takes place here at all. Andrei, the Russian chemist, uses a plastic bottle to draw a water sample from the monastery's well. Then he is given a tiny taste of the matsutake mushrooms that the guide has picked nearby. Matsutake are incredibly valuable delicacies that are said to improve virility, and they are exported to Japan for as much as 1,300 dollars per kilo.

Travelling with us is a cameraman who is filming everything that's happening. We're told it's a service, that we'll be given the opportunity to buy a souvenir DVD of the journey we can show when we get back home, but we know that this is also about surveillance and having pictures that can be used for propaganda. Andrei poses holding a matsutake, and the cameraman eagerly moves around him.

*　*　*

BY THE TIME we are quartered outside a coastal village, night has fallen. We are near the Sea of Japan, which in Korea is called the East Sea. Something that looks like an idyllic village built in a semi-traditional style sits away from a neighbouring settlement. But it was constructed in 2006, the same year as the nuclear weapons test. The guide calls this part of the trip a "home stay" and says that now we're going to make contact with regular North Korean citizens.

Sitting on the veranda of the home of the elderly woman we have been assigned to stay with, we see small wooden boats returning from sea. In the garden, there is an open fire where fish are drying on suspended chicken wire; there is a vegetable plot; a pair of puppies are nipping at each other's ears. The woman squats at the workbench next to the fire and prepares dinner.

We're allocated rooms in a separate part of the house. The woman smiles as she shows us our rooms, but she doesn't speak a word of English. By North Korean standards, these homes are luxurious. Ours has a refrigerator and television, but no running water. A hose runs from a water tank outside the house to the washbasin inside. The smell of fish permeates everything.

We wonder if our hosts always live here, if this is their normal life, or if they are just actors. Why would an elderly woman live in a spacious house alone? This could be the North Korean version of *The Truman Show*, a film where the main character grows up in a small town that's really a giant studio set and he is always followed by a camera. All the houses and buildings are sets, and everyone but Truman is an actor.

In the evening, there's a power outage and everything goes pitch black. When the electricity comes back on after a few hours, a group of military men arrive. We catch a glimpse of them when they sit down in the kitchen, smoking and watching TV.

Our dinner is not served in the house but at a nearby restaurant that is only a few minutes' walk. It's easy to see which dining room is for the North Koreans—rows of shoes are lined up outside the entrance. They eat sitting on the floor, and no meat is served with the kimchi, rice, and vegetables; they have to make do with dried fish. It's also not a restaurant for the villagers—it's for the guides and the chauffeurs. It's made clear to us that there are no other restaurants or bars in the North Korean countryside. When we ask Mr. Song about it, he says that "people prefer to socialize at home."

WE DISCOVER THAT members of the German Friendship Association are in the next room. In many European countries, small Friendship Associations of North Korea were established in the 1970s. Their members believe that everything about North Korea is fantastic, and nothing can change their minds. They aren't allowed to spend time with their Korean brothers, however; instead, they have to endure dining in the tourist section, where we sit at tables in the Western manner, on chairs. We look at the Germans in the adjoining room. They are bearded and wear large sunglasses and knitted vests. They don't look happy.

We don't feel well and leave the rest of the group at the restaurant. Back at the house, food poisoning breaks out with full force. After a few hours, Mr. Song is informed. He is worried and calls a doctor.

The electricity goes off again, and the only source of light is the guide's flashlight. The smell of dried fish is intolerable. A man wearing a cap and no shoes arrives, followed by two women; they give the impression that they've come straight from the fields. The barefoot doctor and his assistants put on white jackets. Then the doctor pulls a blood pressure monitor from his bag. After an examination and a conversation with the guide, the doctor ponders. He explains that our illness is a symptom of shock from coming into contact with Korean culture. One of the nurses takes out a giant syringe. The doctor offers us a shot against culture shock, but we politely decline.

LATER, WE HEAR about the rest of the night at the restaurant. Trond — the large, bald, jovial Norwegian — and the two young farmers from Värmland ordered beer after beer. Soon a squalling, singing gang gathered around Trond. Up until that point, the farmers hadn't said much, but this broke the ice and they joined in the singing. Trond toasted loudly, clinking bottles of Taedong.

The bearded Germans in the next room didn't appreciate the festivities; they wanted the Norwegian and his friends to take it down a notch. It's not appropriate to act like this in North Korea; it's disrespectful. But Trond paid no mind to the buzzkilling requests, until one of them stormed into the room and shouted in English that a spell in a camp would do them good.

It was remarkable that the German sympathizers acknowledged the prison camps — Friends don't tend to broadcast their existence and not much is known about them. There are a few eyewitness accounts, but some of them have been manipulated for South Korean propaganda. It is said that they are in isolated areas, but a number of them are only tens of miles from South Korea, Russia, and China — countries where you can generally move about freely.

A U.S. mapping project called "North Korea Uncovered" has collected testimonies from defectors, investigative reporters, academic texts, accounts from visitors and specialists, and they've studied satellite images and photographs. There is evidence of six camps, totalling 200,000 interned people. According to the project there are two kinds of camps: camps for political prisoners and their families, where most are locked away for life, and camps for criminals who have been tried in court and are serving a sentence. Some camps have both political prisoners and regular criminals.

The German concentration camps weren't unknown during the Second World War. Inspectors arrived and wrote reports about what was going on there. The scope of the extermination wasn't known, but the existence of the camps was. The North Korean work camps, however, don't officially exist according to North Korea. But thanks to Google Earth, anyone with access to the Internet can measure the distance on a satellite image between the village we're staying in and what looks like a gigantic camp facility that is assumed to be "Camp No. 16" — Hwasong concentration camp, the largest in size if not in numbers. Ten thousand prisoners are said to be interned there, forced into slave labour in the underground tunnels where the nuclear testing was carried out. According to a guard who defected from another camp, Hwasong is the most feared of its kind. Those who are considered the most dangerous political opponents are kept there with their families.

On December 20, 2007, 120 prisoners fled from Camp No. 16, according to the Korean evening paper *Daily NK*. By February, twenty-one had been recaptured. None of the remaining escapees managed to get out of the country. We wonder if any of them are still alive, if they are hiding somewhere out there in the night listening to the same cicadas singing in concert.

MORE IS KNOWN about Kwan-li-so 15, the Yoduk concentration camp, than about Hwasong 16. People have managed to escape from Yoduk into neighbouring countries. It is mainly a camp for political prisoners, though calling these inmates "political prisoners" isn't quite accurate. You can land in Yoduk for being at the wrong place at the wrong time, because you've seen too much and know too much. Knowing secrets about the ruling dynasty is especially dangerous. Kim Young-soon, a choreographer who managed to flee the camp and reach South Korea in 2003, gave an account of her experiences to the U.S. Congress in 2011. She had ended up in the Yoduk camp because she knew about Kim Jong-il's relationship with her friend, the actress Song Hye-rim. In 1971 Song, who was North Korea's biggest film star at the time, gave birth to Kim Jong-il's first son, Kim Jong-nam. As long as Kim Il-sung was alive, this out-of-wedlock son was to be kept a secret at all costs. The mere knowledge of his existence led to internment; even the doctor who oversaw the baby's birth was sent to Yoduk. Her whole family was forced to join her.

In her account, Kim Young-soon listed some of the reasons for a person to end up in Yoduk, cases that she learned of from her fellow inmates: breaking a statuette of Kim Jong-il, reproducing a portrait of Kim Il-sung without permission, putting a newspaper featuring Kim Il-sung's picture on the floor, listening to South Korean radio, watching a South Korean film, saying something in casual conversation that could be interpreted as a criticism of the system. Those who report "disloyal citizens" — citizens who have sighed because there is nothing to buy in the store — are considered good and patriotic, and this informant culture depletes social life at the same rate that the political camps are being filled with inmates.

Most of the prisoners aren't told why they have been interned. Allegations aren't read aloud and no trials are held. Many have been sent there because someone in their family is considered untrustworthy. As a relative, you're infected through the bloodline. The family debt isn't arbitrary — it's systematic, and it mirrors the social traditions across Korea, both North and South. One person's actions either honour or dishonour both the immediate family and their relatives, all in accordance with Confucian tradition. In South Korea, petty crimes and corruption aren't particularly dishonourable. The more serious crimes are against one's own family, against the rules of the bloodline: filial piety, duty to your children, securing a family's status, and

42

the children's suitable choice of spouse. In North Korea, the most serious crime one can commit is disloyalty to what you might call the "big family"—that is, the leaders, the party, the state apparatus, and, by extension, the nation. Three generations of a family will be sent to a work camp for disloyalty.

Kim Young-soon was arrested at the central railway station in Pyongyang and taken to a cell that was disguised as a regular apartment in a residential area. She was made to put on a hospital gown and left alone. A mother of four with a newborn, she fainted from the ordeal. She was cared for like a patient by two guards but was given no explanation as to why she was there; the guards didn't ask or answer any questions. Eventually they informed her that she had been sentenced according to a ruling by the party. It was suggested she'd said something that had leaked to South Korea, and shouldn't she take responsibility for that?

Kim wasn't told anything else. She had spent two months under constant supervision, dressed in the hospital gown. Along with her parents and her four children, she was sent to Yoduk. She was told that if she worked hard she would eventually be allowed to leave the camp. If she didn't, she'd be there for the rest of her life.

In *The Aquariums of Pyongyang: Ten Years in the North Korean Gulag* (2001), Kang Chol-hwan recounts his experiences in the same camp, having arrived there as a nine-year-old with his family. They were freed after ten years, and in 1991 Kang managed to get to South Korea, where, with the help of French historian Pierre Rigoulot, he shared his experiences.

His family had chosen to go to North Korea after the Korean War. Kang's grandmother and grandfather grew up on Jeju, a subtropical South Korean island that is now a vacation paradise. Like so many other Koreans, they had sought happiness in Japan during the interwar period. Korea was a Japanese colony that was strictly monitored, but before the Second World War Koreans were not used as slaves in Japan. In the best cases, as with Kang's grandfather, they found success in Japan—some of them even grew wealthy. Kang's grandfather had been made rich by a jewellery business in Kyoto and then found success in the rice trade. But Kang's grandmother was a committed Communist.

During the Korean War, the Korean population in Japan was divided into two political camps: Chongryon, who stood with the Communists in the North, and Mindan, who who allied themselves with the American-supported government in the South. Shortly after the war, North Korea seemed like the better option. With massive Soviet support, manufacturing gained momentum and the people were fed. In the South, on the other hand, poverty was rampant. Furthermore, South Korea granted asylum to those who co-operated with the Japanese colonial power. For Koreans in exile, this was seen as deeply unpatriotic. In contrast, the North seemed like the true Korea, the nation where resistance against the colonizers was pure and uncorrupted.

Kang's grandmother convinced her husband to take the

boat to Pyongyang with the rest of their family. Kang's grandfather took his Volvo on the boat, where they were given special treatment because of his wealth.

But North Korea wasn't the paradise that the Chongryon organization had depicted. People monitored each other, all information was restricted, and dejection hung over Pyongyang. When they tried to take a road trip to explore the areas outside the city, they were immediately stopped by the military. Free travel in the country was unheard of.

It wasn't many years until the Volvo was handed over as a gift to the party. First it was suggested, then it was recommended, and then came a final order. Still, these were happy years compared to their time in the camp. Kang's grandparents held administrative posts within the bureaucracy and the union, and they lived in one of the better areas of Pyongyang.

Kang was born in 1967 and he had a rather happy, carefree childhood in the city. He liked to fight and to wind up the children of the Soviet diplomat living in the neighbourhood. Aquarium fish were his great passion.

One day, in 1977, Kang's grandfather didn't come home from work. He was never seen again. Shortly after, the police came to pick up the rest of the family, except Kang's mother. They were taken to Yoduk. Apparently, their crime was Kang's grandfather's inability to fit in.

FOR TEN YEARS the family toiled in the camp. Prisoners worked in agriculture, mining, and industrial manufacturing. Kang's uncle, a trained chemist, was allowed to work in a distillery. The children went to school. All the guards, teachers, and functionaries also lived in the area with their families.

Corporal punishment and humiliation are part of daily life and are dealt out both methodically and arbitrarily. Escape attempts have only one punishment: public execution. All the prisoners are forced to watch the hangings. Two to three thousand prisoners are made to chant "Death to the people's enemies" in unison while throwing stones at the bodies. Kang wrote that many of the newly arrived shut their eyes during the stoning.

Sex and love between prisoners is almost as serious a crime as an escape attempt. Women who get pregnant are publicly humiliated by being forced to describe in detail how the act of love unfolded. (For Kang these situations served the dual purpose of a punishment and a kind of sex education.) Pregnant women are forced to have abortions. If that doesn't work and the child is born anyway, the newborn is taken away from the mother at birth, never to be seen again. The children are considered carriers of their parents' disloyalty. The bloodline has to be severed.

One form of punishment for men is the so-called "sweat box," a windowless isolation cell in which the occupant can barely move. Food rations are reduced, and so the prisoner is forced to eat insects in order to survive. After enduring this treatment, the captive crawls out on all fours looking like a living skeleton. That is, Kang recounts, if he survives his time in the box.

WHEN THE GERMAN Friendship Association filed out of the restaurant, each and every one of them was glowing with ire—dark-eyed, teeth grinding, mumbling curses as they disappeared into the darkness. The Hwasong concentration camp is forty-five kilometres away. If the Germans had their way, it might have been a short ride for Trond and the Värmlanders.

DAY 3

STRONG WATER

Madame choi's time in captivity was luxurious compared to life in a work camp. In the villa there were no locks on the doors, but she felt as if she were always being watched. She had long been accustomed to a hectic working life; now she didn't have much to do. The days stretched out aimlessly. During the first six months, she could only manage to eat one bowl of *jook* (rice porridge) each day.

Kim Jong-il's Friday-night movie screenings and the parties that followed were the only activities that interrupted her ennui. At these events, a selection of films from the leader's private archives was shown to a circle of dignitaries. As soon as the guests arrived, they had to partake in a ritual: knocking back a large glass of cognac. Madame had to wear a *joseonot*, the traditional dress, at these parties. That was all. She simply had to be there, appearing as if she'd stepped right out of the silver screen.

Each screening was followed by games of backgammon and mah-jong, punctuated by more large snifters of cognac, which were downed while standing. Kim Jong-il thought the true nature of proselytizers emerged when they were drunk. Then there was dancing to an all-female band that played jazz and disco. In the wee hours of the morning, Kim Jong-il took the stage to conduct this lady orchestra.

ON MAY 10, Madame Choi was invited to Kim Jong-il's first-born son's birthday. This was the child born out of wedlock who had earned the obstetrician and the lover's friend places in the work camp. He was turning seven.

The leader had six televisions in his office. One of them was tuned to a South Korean channel. At the birthday dinner, Madame met Kim Jong-il's wife, who differed from other women she had seen in North Korea. The wife had permed hair and dressed with a Western sensibility. Apparently, she'd accepted Kim Jong-il's illegitimate son.

Kim Jong-il talked about film throughout the meal. He harped on about how "the evil North Korean leaders" were portrayed in South Korean TV series. After dinner, Madame's domestic was beside herself about the invitation to the birthday party. It was unreal, an unbelievable gesture, the domestic said.

In September, after having been at the villa for half a year, Madame was woken in the middle of the night. She shook with fear, thinking that she was going to be executed. But then it was explained to her that she was simply being moved to another house, because the villa was needed for a number of foreign guests who had arrived to celebrate the thirtieth anniversary of the birth of the nation. They packed up quickly, drove through the night, and finally arrived at a more modest house in the country.

After a few weeks, she was asked to write her life story. Only important people were asked to write their memoirs, it was explained, so she should consider the task an honour. After hesitating, she agreed and decided to be honest. When her account was read, it was cause for concern: her mind was thoroughly corrupted by imperialist dogma.

That was the end of the invitations to parties with Pyong-yang's elite. Madame's mind needed to be cleansed with lessons on revolutionary history and Juche, the North Korean ideology. For five hours a day, three days a week, she studied Juche. On Fridays there was a test.

THE YEARS PASSED and Choi Eun-hee filled her days with gardening. She sculpted small clay cranes, which she placed in the garden with their beaks pointing south. In her autobiography *Gobaek*, she recounts how she was forced to write to Kim Il-sung, sending her congratulations on his birthday. She was shown how the letter should begin, how a decent address should look:

In the history of humanity, you most superior, radiant, honourable, creator of the eternal, indestructible Juche Thought. Great Leader, powerful ideological theorist who led two victorious revolutionary wars against Japan and America, who gloriously established independence and achieved racial honour. Initiator, eternally victorious, brilliant Iron-Willed Commander, in revolution and in enforcement, founder of an international example, liberator from colonialism and liberator in the history of the world, you eternally brilliant, invaluable, and highest, who laid out our ingenious revolutionary strategies, Beloved Leader, comrade Kim Il-sung...

Madame Choi was unaware that her ex-husband Shin Sang-ok was in the country at this time. The director was also quartered in a villa, but after five months he tried to escape. He stole a car and drove until the gas ran out, reached a train station by foot, and there he hid in a storeroom filled with explosives. He snuck onto a freight train but was discovered the next morning. After being arrested, he endured a lengthy interrogation in which the guards asked him a question and then left the room when he answered, only to return after they'd consulted with Kim Jong-il on the phone.

Shin was locked in an isolation cell for three months. He tried to escape again, but was caught. This time he was formally tried and charged. He was sent to a prison, where he was put through a rigorous re-education program and made to do intense physical exercises. The guards also told him that Madame Choi had died in North Korea, and he mourned her. He tried to go on a hunger strike but violence was used to force him to eat. They said he was the first person ever to be forced to eat. He must have been an important prisoner.

Shin was made to write long, remorseful letters to Kim Jong-il, explaining that he was ready to be of service to the revolution. These correspondences had the same tone as the congratulatory letter Madame Choi wrote to Kim Il-sung.

And then, one day, he was set free. It was February 1983.

*   *   *

COME MORNING, WE are sore and drained from the previous day's bus trip and the terrors of last night. The Norwegian and his gang are hungover. Others have also been sick to their stomachs. Andrei spent the entire night vomiting after tasting his first-ever matsutake. Earlier this morning, someone saw Ms. Kim tottering onto the beach in her high heels and dress to throw up. Now, all we have to look forward to are hours on the bumpy roads back to the airbase.

We walk toward the beach and pass the gravel road where members of the Korean Youth Corps, in their white shirts and red kerchiefs, are cycling to school. A long avenue of poplars with white-painted trunks leads to an unusual concrete bunker, reminiscent of a modernist beach house in an Antonioni film. A truck carrying uniformed workers passes us. The workers are standing up straight on the bed, close together; they stare gravely at us.

We aren't allowed to travel beyond the concrete bunker—that's crossing the line. Elias made an attempt to walk to a village farther along but was immediately stopped by a guard. He was given various explanations: there were roadworks; it might be dangerous for him because he doesn't speak Korean. When these unlikely explanations were left hanging in the air, he was told that these were military orders.

The morning light is mild and the winds are pleasant down by the sea. We swim and the water is so salty that it lifts us to the surface. As we dry ourselves in the sun, Mr. Song comes walking by. He spends some time skipping rocks with us. When we turn around we see that the cameraman has just captured this scene of unforced fellowship between nations.

THE BUS SHUDDERS along the potholed roads. It takes six hours to reach Orang, and Mr. Song suggests that we should kill time by singing. Ms. Kim turns out to have the voice of an angel. She glows and sparkles as she and Andrei sing a few traditional Russian folk songs.

Andrei sits with his computer in his lap. Looking somewhat rumpled, he studies his music downloads. For some reason he has songs by various Swedish Eurovision contestants — Carola, Tommy Körberg — and ABBA's collected works. He pulls out a bundle of lyrics from his luggage and chooses a song by Baccara, the Spanish disco-queen duo who were in their prime around the same time as Madame Choi was kidnapped. He picks up the microphone with his eyes glued to the paper. In a low voice, he sings the disco queen's lyrics about love and ecstasy.

Andrei's song seems to go on and on forever.

*　*　*

IN THE ANTONOV, we fly northwest to Ryanggang Province, a mountainous region that borders China. We land at Samjiyon Airport, which was built by a South Korean company in the 1980s, when there were ideas about expanding the tourism industry. Samjiyon was supposed to be a ski resort, but the South Koreans pulled out, leaving behind an asphalt square in a coniferous forest.

The three young men from Bromma in our group appear to be in high school. Their hair is shoulder-length, the collars of their polo shirts are popped, and they're wearing sports shorts and deck shoes. Why they chose to take a trip to North Korea is a mystery. For a moment, we wonder if the trip is part of hazing at one of Stockholm's better schools.

Our bags are loaded onto a trailer attached to a very small, bright red, antique tractor. The boys guffaw as the contraption sputters off toward a simple building that functions as a waiting room. The driver, who has a weather-beaten face and wears a brown uniform and a wide cap, drives his vehicle off unperturbed. Blue-black smoke puffs from the little exhaust, which looks like an organ pipe.

THE BUS DRIVES us through the forest on gravel roads. Like the other buses, this one is adorned with a red sign that announces that we are "foreigners." A few of the people walking along the road look at us curiously; many hide their faces. Some rush right out into the trees as we near.

We've started to stake out our seats on the bus already. At the front is Oksana, who talks endlessly to those around her. Those who've gone one round with her are happy to switch places. The Russian chemist and his personal guide, Ms. Kim, are also at the front. She is forced to endure his gentle stench. The smell is contained when Andrei sits still, but it's released when he makes certain sudden movements. A piercing waft slips from his collar, as if he were hiding goat cheese under his shirt. We've also found ourselves close to the front, along with the Gothenburger who lives in Minsk and the tattooed baker, but at a safe distance from Oksana's incessant chatter. The baker is having some stomach trouble. He kills the dead time by reading various issues of *World Wildlife* magazine from front to back. He's currently engrossed in an article about lemurs. The Värmlanders seem like they're fused together; one never leaves the other's side and both barely say a word. They have found their place in the middle together with the pilot, Trond, and the enormous Swiss, Bruno. Farther back is Ari, with his camera equipment; he has a freshly roused look on his face and wears a flat cap askew. Farthest back are the guys from the posh Stockholm suburb, who we've started to call "the Bromma boys."

Elias moves around the back of the bus and delivers short, spontaneous lectures. He's a living encyclopedia on North Korea. He's read the foreign policy editorials and the stories of defectors; he follows all of the blogs; he knows everything about the ruling dynasty's family tree and about the diplomats' hardships in Pyongyang. The Bromma boys listen with amusement.

Elias talks about the North Koreans' language. In their

dialect, foreign words are avoided. Words borrowed from English are extremely rare, but certain Russian words are part of the vocabulary. All this in accordance with the idea that self-reliance is an essential national trait. South Korean comedy shows sometimes poke fun at the way those in the North speak. Not least, they laugh at the clumsy soccer referees whose words for things like "forward" and "offside" become long, swollen phrases.

But certain words in North Korea have retained meanings that are lost in the South. Madame Choi writes in her autobiography that during her time in confinement she had a guide who sometimes brought her along to shop for necessities. On one occasion, the guide asked for a *bulal* in a store. "*Bulal*" in South Korean means "testicle"; in North Korea it still means "lightbulb."

THE CLIMATE IS different at this altitude — much cooler — and the flora reminds us of early autumn in Värmland, with yellow-hued birch trees shading the dense forest.

We are taken to a clearing, much bigger than the airport and paved with stone. A gigantic, gleaming bronze statue of Kim Il-sung reigns over the landscape. This statue could easily be in a square in a large city, with giant spotlights lining the pavement to illuminate the scene at night. But, instead, it sits in the middle of a forest.

The statue, called the *Samjiyon Grand Monument*, is supposed to depict the leader during a guerilla attack against Japan. He holds a pair of binoculars in one hand and is backed by four relief groups sculpted in the same social realist style, depicting enthusiastic followers: "On the Field," "The Motherland," "Yearning," and "Forward." The leader's body language radiates resourcefulness and decisiveness, but his face has a softness, a touch of the Buddha.

THE AMERICAN ANTHROPOLOGIST Roy Richard Grinker says that Kim Il-sung is supposed to resemble a mother figure as much as he does a father figure. In North Korean news articles and stories, he's often described as feminine in his ways: maternal, caring, and gentle. Far from Stalin's massive, masculine, frightening scowl, Kim Il-sung's made-up face is round and has dimples. It is the inviting, relaxed face of a person who is far too good, who spoils his own.

In *The Cleanest Race*, the American author B. R. Myers builds on this idea, suggesting that the representations of Kim Il-sung as the country's mother were later transferred to Kim Jong-il. He was The Son, but he also became the country's new or parallel Mother through a remarkable transformation: he became a new mother who lives side by side with the elder patriarch/matriarch. In October 2003, the North Korean state declared: "Let the imperialist enemies come at us with their nuclear weapons, for there is no power on earth that can defeat our strength and love and the power of our belief, which thanks to the blood bond between mother and child create a fortress of single-heartedness. Our Great Mother, General Kim Jong-il!"

IN HIS FINAL years, Kim Il-sung was plagued by a tumour the size of an orange on the side of his neck. Among the malnourished, these tumours—calcium deposits—aren't uncommon. In North Korea they are called *hok*. Doctors didn't dare operate on the leader because the growth was too close to his spinal cord and brain. But all photography of that side of him was forbidden, and on official occasions his bodyguards arranged themselves so as to block its view.

In a Swedish national radio documentary by Lovisa Lamm, the Swedish diplomat Lars Bergqvist describes how he briefly met Kim Il-sung in the 1980s. He talks about how he couldn't take his eyes off the enormous tumour, "which was also covered in hair."

After the meeting, he said to the North Korean chief of protocol: "It's very interesting to meet Kim Il-sung, but that was a terrible growth he had. Shouldn't it be removed?"

"Which growth?" the functionary replied. "No, he doesn't have a tumour, it doesn't exist."

Bergqvist understood that the thing was unmentionable and wrapped up the conversation. "All right then, let's leave it at that."

The tumour could have been seen as a mark of nobility, proof of the simple roots that Kim Il-sung transcended. But not at that size. It ruined all that was inviting—those defined eyebrows and the symmetry of his peach-like cheeks.

As a parental figure, Kim Il-sung is a synthesis of mother and father in the eyes of his citizens. The Korean word *"oboi"* (parent), which is most often used about the leader, is just a compound of the words *"ob"* (mother) and *"oi"* (father). In the large mosaics and cult imagery depicting the leader, his wife is seldom by his side. Mother/Father Kim Il-sung doesn't need a woman, and all the citizens in the country are his children. In TV interviews at schools and orphanages, the children call Kim Il-sung "Father." In *Korea and Its Futures*, Roy Richard Grinker describes a South Korean television spot in which a young North Korean boy is snacking on sweets. A Japanese journalist asks who gave him the candy, and the boy replies: "From the Great Leader, my father."

There are many stories, most of them from the KCNA, about how during a catastrophe the first things regular North Korean citizens rescue are portraits of the leader. After the floods that plagued the country in 1997, the KCNA reported: "When the water drained away in the areas that were hit, people were found buried in the clay and sand. Clutched to their chests were portraits carefully wrapped in plastic."

WE ARE ENCOURAGED to buy a bouquet of cloth flowers that some uniformed women are selling. They are the only people around. Then we are lined up and asked to bow before the statue, and a representative of the group approaches the pedestal and lays down the flowers. We are slightly embarrassed when we bow, but none of us protest. We're being incorporated into North Korea's choreography.

After a short walk in the afternoon sun by the mirror-like Lake Samji, where we see small squirrels scurrying in the balsam poplars, we notice that the bouquet we bought and placed at the foot of the statue is being offered for sale again. But we don't see any new customers.

* * *

BACK ON THE bus, Mr. Song tries to explain to us what Juche means and how the unique ideology gives the country direction, but it's all very abstract and we aren't any the wiser. In English, the word is sometimes translated as "self-reliance." The Juche ideology is often described as a mix of Stalinism and Confucianism, but above all of isolationism and archaistic, pan-Korean nationalism. Juche can also be seen as part of a Holy Trinity where Kim Il-sung is the Father, Kim Jong-il is the Son, and Juche is the Holy Ghost. Since Kim Il-sung launched the term, this "truth of truths," as it is written on the Tower of the Juche Idea in Pyongyang, has taken hold in all imaginable areas of North Korean society. Its huge influence is most likely connected to the permanent state of emergency that the country is in — answering a need for security that has deep historical roots and was dramatically realized during the Korean War.

The American bombardment of North Korea during the Korean War was an inexorable, drawn-out war crime. Almost everything was a legitimate target: all means of communication, roads, bridges, and all productive entities — every factory, rice field, city, and village. The Americans deployed napalm and experimented with biological warfare by using insects that spread anthrax and bubonic plague. North Koreans grew accustomed to living in constant fear of bombing and spent their lives underground, where they built homes, schools, hospitals, and factories. With Hiroshima and Nagasaki fresh in their minds, they were convinced that one of the planes would be carrying a nuclear bomb.

To endure and then overcome those circumstances was something of a miracle. According to North Korean mythology it was thanks to the resourcefulness of one single man — Kim Il-sung, the Great Leader — that the country emerged victorious from the war. Using his exploits as a leitmotif, the Juche idea of taking control of your circumstances — taking care of yourself and being suspicious of the world around you — took root.

ONE FACET OF this concept of self-reliance is usually traced back to Korea's historical practice of isolation. During the latter part of the Joseon dynasty (1392–1897), the West referred to Korea as the "Hermit Kingdom," a term that has since been assimilated in South Korea and used in the country's own historical accounts. Korea was a nation cloaked in myth. As the story goes, the kingdom didn't even take in castaways; instead, they were held in the harbours only to be deported as quickly as possible. Others weren't allowed to leave the country at all. In 1653 Hendrick Hamel, the first Westerner ever to write about Korea, landed there after his vessel, which belonged to the Dutch East India Company, was shipwrecked near Jeju Island. The thirty-six survivors weren't allowed to leave the country because it was feared that they would reveal the secret of the kingdom's existence to the rest of the world. After thirteen years, Hamel and seven other crew members managed to escape.

Whereas Japan allowed some of its harbours to be forced open for trade in the 1850s, following violent threats by the

Americans, Korea's response to the same tactic was to sink the American naval fleet and kill the crew. This incident, as well as the self-containment that dominated the Joseon period, has been highlighted in the retelling of the story of Korea, pushing other, equally valid variations into the shadows. Accounts of Korean history could just as well focus on the generous immigration laws during the Goryeo dynasty (918–1392) or when Korea acted as a safe haven for refugees from Manchuria and China at the end of the Second World War.

Historically, the primary frame of reference for Korea has been China, which for periods of time it was linked to as a vassal state. The Japanese colonial period from 1910–1945 is actually just a historical parenthesis. Still, one cannot deny that parts of North Korea have been unusually isolated. It's possible that certain areas have never been seen by Westerners and, with the exception of the odd Japanese colonial functionary, never by another foreigner in modern times.

AT A MEETING in May 2006 between the South and North Korean militaries, the South's representative mentioned that it was normal for South Korean farmers to marry foreign women from Vietnam, the Philippines, and Mongolia. In the countryside at the time, the population was declining. With more efficient farming methods reducing the number of agricultural workers needed, and new generations of women moving away from rural areas to receive an education, many farmers found it difficult to find a Korean partner. And the educated Korean women were also struggling to find a suitable match—a popular topic of discussion in the South Korean media, along with the extremely low birth rate.

The North Korean representative interrupted his colleague: "Our nation has always considered its pure lineage to be of great importance. I am concerned that our singularity will disappear."

The South Korean answered that the number of foreigners "was a mere drop of ink in the Han River"—the Han being the river that cuts through Seoul.

The serviceman from the North replied: "Not even one drop of ink must be allowed to fall into the Han River."

The North Korean leaders took advantage of the conformist tradition in Korea and used pictures and stories to create the national myth of a "child race"—natural, clean, impulsive, guided by a lovable leader. To a great extent, the myths and attitudes of Japanese fascism were adopted more than those of Confucianism and Communism. The colour white was adopted as a symbol of purity: the white uniforms, the white snow, the white horses.

In contrast to many other analysts, B. R. Myers dismissed the idea of Confucianism's presence in North Korea. The proof is in the synthesis of mother and father in the figure of the leader. To elevate the mother in this way goes totally against Confucian traditions, which teach that a mother is subordinate even to her sons. In *The Cleanest Race*, Myers even rejects referring to North Korea as a "hard-line Stalinist state" because the racial theorizing that dominates the country can't be equated to Communist ideology, which emphasizes internationalism. During the Cold War, North Korea was the black sheep in the Communist community because of its unusual interpretation of Communism. In the end it was only China that really accepted North Korea, and this was for the pragmatic reason of wanting to maintain the status quo of their fragile relationship.

Myers calls Juche Thought a "sham doctrine" and gives a number of reasons for its introduction. Like all leaders and prophets sent by the divine, Kim Il-sung needed his own ideology—no less would do for a man put on such a high pedestal. Most likely because the dynastic structure of North Korean society was difficult to reconcile with Marxism, there was also an ideological need to create distance from the Communist body of thought and maybe an even greater need to obscure the country's actual system of belief—the nationalist race doctrine that has characterized North Korea since its founding.

Analysts agree that Hwang Jang-yop, a philosophy teacher at Kim Il-sung University, was the architect of Juche Thought. Hwang was Kim Jong-il's philosophy teacher but fell out of favour with the leadership in the 1980s. On a trip back from Japan in 1997, he escaped to Beijing and thus became the highest-level party functionary to have defected from North Korea. He later settled in South Korea and devoted himself to criticizing Kim Jong-il's feudal regime, even testifying about the violence and famine in North Korea.

Myers says that the Juche texts are self-consciously jumbled and that they resemble "a college student trying to both stretch a term paper to a respectable length and to discourage anyone from reading it through." The texts have a special function: to be harmless, impenetrable, and abrasive all at once. Still, it seems like Hwang Jang-yop truly believed in Juche Thought, however dubious it seemed. While under constant threat of assassination by agents from the North Korean secret police, he accused Kim Jong-il of having betrayed and corrupted Juche ideology. He recommended a rock-solid policy of ostracization against the North, saying it would lead to the collapse of the country, and suggested that he himself would be ready to take over as the leader of an interim government should such a time come.

Privately, Hwang Jang-yop suffered greatly. His wife, whom he left in North Korea, committed suicide; one daughter died under mysterious circumstances, and his other children ended up in work camps.

IN *THE CLEANEST RACE*, B. R. Myers emphasizes that Juche Thought gave North Korean suspicion and self-reliance a loose ideological framework — and that it essentially must be viewed as a racist teaching built on notions of blood mysticism. The North Korean race doctrine may be extreme, but the idea of pure blood is strong throughout the peninsula. Even in the South, mixing blood is still seen by many as shameful and threatening. In fact South Korea cultivates the notion of being the most genetically homogenous country in the world, disregarding the "genetic influx" from China, Japan, and Okinawa. Such great weight has been placed on this idea of blood that South Korean citizens have not been allowed to do military service if they have a non-Korean parent. Their anomalous skin colour would make it hard for such soldiers to "mix with their Korean colleagues in the barracks," said a representative from the Ministry of Defence in an article in the *Korea Times*.

In Korea, the question of blood ties is linked to the violence the country experienced during the Japanese colonization that lasted until the end of the Second World War. The Japanese army had a comprehensive system for forcefully recruiting "comfort women," which was the term used for "sex slaves."

Choi Eun-hee's parents tried to marry her off very young so she wouldn't be "recruited" as a sex slave. She was a tomboy at heart but was considered very beautiful and was, like so many other women, at risk. Her grandmother said, with a note of incantation: "You are a little girl with long eyelashes. The kind that sleeps a lot."

Madame's own solution was to find work at a theatre as a teenager — work that was considered as lowly as a shaman's, circus artist's, or *gisaeng*'s (geisha's), but that protected her from sexual slavery. The reason was, of course, not only to avoid becoming a comfort woman, but because she was drawn to the theatre. To everyone's surprise — she was a shy girl — she was a natural actor. Her father was opposed to it and tried to lock her up at home. But her will was too strong. She escaped to the stage.

UNSURPRISINGLY, RESEARCHERS AREN'T in agreement about the statistics, but from a Korean perspective the

Imperial Japanese Army forcefully recruited around 200,000 Korean women as sex slaves. The issue is still incredibly charged, and those who want to approach it in South Korea must do so with great care. In 2004, the TV star Lee Seung-yeon had a hit with Kim Ki-duk's film *3-Iron*. Like so many other television stars, she decided to crown her career with a pin-up calendar featuring pictures of her, scantily clad, in exotic environs. The PR company that was brought on board booked a photographer who took a few promotional shots of Lee posing as a "comfort woman" on the Palau islands in the Pacific Ocean (Palau was one of the places where sex slaves were taken during the Second World War). The photographs were presented at a press conference and the reaction in South Korea was huge. After angry protests broke out, Lee went to visit an old-age home for former sex slaves, where she begged for mercy on bare knees. The head of the PR firm had his head shaved in front of the media, an action of regret and submission. But the public wasn't satisfied until the photographer had burned the negatives on a public square in Seoul.

*　*　*

IT'S EVENING AT the hotel outside of Samjiyon. We're sitting on our beds, waiting for the hot water to be turned on. During dinner, Mr. Song had explained that we should avoid brushing our teeth with the tap water.

"The water is very *strong*," he said. "You might lose all of your teeth."

67

Andrei, the Russian chemist, perked up when he heard Ms. Kim's translation of the warning. He was looking forward to collecting yet another unique water sample to take back to Moscow.

"Awesome, now I'm going to lose my teeth," one of the Bromma boys grumbled. He'd already used the strong tap water.

In anticipation of the hot water that comes on for only one hour a day, we watch scenes from parliament on the national television channel. The camera pans slowly over the rows of ageing men and the occasional woman, who all sit with their eyes shut as if lost in prayer. Sometimes a concise, low chant breaks out in response to the speaker's sermon-like statements. Along with Kim Jong-il, the 687 representatives in the Supreme People's Assembly are actually elected. And as nominated representatives they always get 100 percent of the votes "from the people." When measures come up for vote in the assembly, the members always hold up their cards openly. They are always in agreement with their leader. It is as if they are the nervous system and he is the brain.

After the long-winded political liturgy comes a film showing archival footage narrated by a man with a hysterical voice. People toil in the fields, in the steel mills, on the railroads, on the rice paddies. Physical labour is undertaken by smiling citizens who move like wind-up toys.

The narrator goes up in pitch and the scene shifts to a group of people pulling a boat to shore during a storm. They throw themselves at the rope, eyes ablaze, someone falls but clambers up again, laughing. Kim Jong-il shows up in the next scene, and the narrator is on the verge of collapse, blubbering with tears and giddy laughter. When the leader is not shaking hands, he's gesturing with his right hand with soft, fast movements, giving instructions about everything imaginable. This "on-the-spot guidance" happens wherever he is, whether it's in an office or on the factory floor. Now a blushing woman poses by his side. She takes his arm and giggles. It's a heated moment — something unrestrained is breaking through.

We stare at the images of Kim Jong-il on the television. Then a montage shows the launching of a Taepodong missile, followed by people's reactions to the announcement of the new weapon. The footage shows people reading the newspapers and cheering; there are close-ups of others who are mad with joy. They bounce up and down, arms raised, eyes shining. The narrator is ecstatic.

The pipes cough. The hour of hot water has begun.

THE MONSTER

I N THE MORNING, distant rhythmic howls can be heard in the surrounding woods. We're sitting in the bus outside of the hotel, waiting for everyone else in the group to turn up. Assuming they've survived the strong water, that is. The hotel personnel, who act more like functionaries, won't let us leave. They've discovered that four towels embellished with tigers are missing. They have even identified the guilty among us, but none of those who are named will admit to towel theft. The Värmlanders are silent as stone and stare out at the spruce forest. The Ukrainian wearing camouflage pants denies it flat out, and the Bromma boys don't even bother responding. But the functionaries insist. In the end, Trond tires of the fuss, and goes in and pays the twenty-four dollars for the four tiger towels.

The incident has delayed us and it jeopardizes our visit to the first stop on the day's schedule: the Samjiyon

Schoolchildren's Palace. Andrei has a framed certificate of friendship from the Russian Academy of Sciences in Moscow that he is supposed to present to the representatives of the after-school facility.

In Samjiyon we pass a group of uniformed workers who march in lines of two, their shovels over their shoulders. A red banner has been mounted on the main street. Preparations are underway for the sixtieth-anniversary celebration of the nation. The high, peaked roofs of the residences resemble gingerbread houses, likely a design element related to the area's intended status as a ski resort. But there are also rows of white-painted houses made of armoured concrete that look like they could withstand almost anything.

Mr. Song is stressed out. He explains that we don't have time to get off at the schoolchildren's palace. But the bus travels up the driveway to the front of the building and Andrei jumps off the bus with the certificate tucked under his arm. He rushes up the stairs, manages to shake hands with a man wearing a suit, hands over the frame, and runs back. The bus is already moving when he throws himself back on board. We see the disappointed man on the stairs awkwardly waving us off.

BUT THERE IS no time to dwell on this. We have more important things ahead of us. We are on our way to Baekdu, the holy revolutionary mountain — a dormant volcano with a crater lake. The bus travels along gravel roads through spruce forests. As we ascend the mountain, larch forests take over, the trees become more gnarled and sparse, and the air is ever cooler. The landscape is more barren the higher up we go, and soon a wooded upland with mighty views unfurls before us.

Baekdu is the highest point on the entire Korean peninsula. The rusty red and orange streaks of lava on the volcanic rock remind us of Iceland's landscape. The haze between the distant, bluish ridges of Manchuria creates a depth of field like stained glass. Snow leopards, wild boar, wolves, bears, and even the Siberian tiger—here called the Baekdu tiger—are said to still roam this land.

In 1999, North Korea gifted a Baekdu tiger to South Korea as a gesture of reconciliation. The renowned South Korean stem cell researcher Hwang Woo-suk immediately began a cloning project to preserve the Baekdu tiger's Korean origin. "I'll spread the Korean people's spirit by cloning the Mount Baekdu tiger," he proclaimed. But this was before Hwang claimed to have cloned human stem cells and was exposed for having fabricated his results. Since that scandal, South Korean stem cell research has had to live down a bad reputation.

We ascend to a plateau, pass by a military checkpoint, and make our way to the volcano by foot. When we get to the ridge of the crater we look out over the magnificent crater lake. Cheonji—Heaven Lake—is majestic, with its cerulean water. When we look across the rim of the volcano—at a distance of about five kilometres—we spot the Chinese border control, which looks like a set of small nesting boxes atop a mountain.

To celebrate Kim Il-sung's eighty-second birthday,

enormous metal letters that spelled out "revolutionary holy mountain" were set into the slope. Over a three-year period, the letters and the amenities on Baekdu were built by so-called "shock brigades." It was heroic work, and the suffering itself had value. According to the Workers' Party of North Korea's publication *Rodong Sinmun* (*Workers' Newspaper*), the shock brigade "dragged huge tree trunks down the mountainsides" and "gathered stones from the beds of rivers where ice was floating."

Baekdu occupies a central place in North Korea's national mythology. The iconography of the mountain is spread through depictions on photographs, stamps, mosaics, and paintings. The revolutionary Korean spirit — the one that drove out the Japanese colonizers and triumphed over the imperialists — radiates from the volcano like the aura of a giant magical monolith.

According to the official national legend, Kim Jong-il was born in a little wooden cabin just down the mountain. At the moment of his birth, a bright new star appeared in the sky, along with a double rainbow, if one can imagine these two phenomena occurring simultaneously. Then, as Bertil Lintner recounts in *Great Leader, Dear Leader*, a swallow descended from the heavens to "herald the birth of a general who will rule all the world." When Kim Jong-il returned to his birthplace for the first time in his adult life, a similar natural phenomenon happened: the heavy clouds hanging over the crater scattered and a rainbow stretched across the heavens. The elements acknowledged him as the master.

A guide wearing a brown uniform and a peaked cap

speaks to us using a megaphone. She gestures with her arms, explaining that the peaks of the holy revolutionary mountain are always covered in snow. When we point at the mountain and tell the guide that they aren't actually covered in snow, she looks past us and repeats: "The peaks of holy revolutionary mountain are always covered in snow." The observations of us mere civilians are not to sully the image of this national treasure, whose prescribed appearance is inscribed in the nation's history forever.

IN 1935, THE Swedish explorer Sten Bergman was one of the few Western travellers to visit the Baekdu region. With him was his entourage: Harald Sjökvist, a taxidermist and former locomotive driver, and Kenji Fujimoto, a Japanese chef and Casanova. Bergman found fresh tracks from a pack of wolves, and he caught a Ural owl, a three-toed woodpecker, a black woodpecker, an azure-winged magpie, and a black grouse. Bergman also photographed the people he met on his journey. The birds are in the Swedish Museum of Natural History's collections in Stockholm, and the photographs are today considered unique documents. In Bergman's time, this region was largely untraversable. Under normal circumstances, the explorer claimed, you would be robbed, killed, or kidnapped by Manchurian or Korean bandits. He and his companions had once found a dead Korean on a mountain slope but they themselves survived thanks to their military escort of fifty Japanese soldiers. In his book, *In Korean Wilds and Villages*, he writes:

Clouds of mist now came sweeping along and hid parts of the lake, but at moments they would clear off and we could again see the whole of it. Swifts bred in great numbers in the crevices of the crater walls and we could see many of them as they swept through the air. There was a sharp wind and it was bitterly cold. Gusts of sand also kept blowing about...

On a level plateau right on the highest point of the mountain a ceremony was now to take place. The trumpet-call went forth to summon all together, and the military formed rank in perfect style, facing toward Japan. The other members of the expedition also formed themselves into a group alongside. With fixed bayonets and drawn swords, the following words were then called out with wild enthusiasm: "*Tenno heika bansai, Kogo heika bansai!*" — "Long live His Majesty the Emperor, Long live Her Majesty the Empress!"

Our group stands in formation against the background of the crater lake. The sand whirls and the calls of swifts echo in the crevices of the crater walls. The man who films us takes a group photo.

Swiss Bruno leads a hike up to the very top — a cliff formation that juts out over one side and has no safety railings. Bruno quickly pulls ahead of the group. He moves with incredible determination. Behind him are the Swedish fighter pilot and the Värmlanders. The rest of us taste blood in our mouths and our breathing is laboured in the thin air. We are at an elevation of 2,700 metres.

After climbing to the summit, we don't join those from the group who decide to take a cable car down to the lake. Instead we stare at a dangerously steep stairway that runs halfway down to the water and watch Andrei taking another water sample. It's hard to imagine that this cold lake can accommodate any life, but after being stocked with fish in the 1960s it is now home to a subspecies of Arctic char. In 1987, a splendid specimen was caught during test fishing. It was put on ice and flown to Kim Jong-il's palace, where it was served at his birthday dinner.

We've been told that the treacherous stairway is made up of 216 steps, a numerological representation of Kim Jong-il's birthday (February 16). Uncharacteristically, they underestimated the numbers. There are surely several thousand steps and it is so steep that even the least afflicted might get vertigo.

The heavenly lake is deep. At its deepest, it's nearly 400 metres to the bottom. Since 1903, there have been regular reports from the Chinese side that the lake is home to a monster, and in more recent years, film footage and photographs have been presented as evidence of its existence. The monster was described as having a long neck and a bull-like head when it was first sighted, and was said to have attacked people at the water's edge; they responded with six shots from a gun and the creature fled back to the depths of the lake. Other eyewitness accounts describe an animal that resembles a giant seal, with a long neck and a human head. The most recent report was in 2007, when a Chinese TV reporter filmed a twenty-minute sequence that captured six creatures swimming in formation. Judging by the trails in the water and what appeared to be heads breaking the water's surface, this footage appeared to show large animals of some kind. Their fins, or wings, were longer than their bodies, the reporter said, and they swam as fast as motorboats.

But there is no room in the North Korean historical record for a monster dwelling in the depths of Heaven Lake. It is not denied that there are large animals living in the lake, however: the Arctic char must have mutated into giant fish over time.

BEFORE WE LEAVE Mount Baekdu we meet a group of uniformed men and women, some of whom are carrying red flags. They look important in their caps, with their stern expressions, but when the guard sounds his whistle they rush back. It turns out they are regular workers being ordered to the top of the mountain, where they have a job to do.

*　*　*

IT IS ALMOST thirty-seven years to the day that three Swedish leftist radicals were invited to visit North Korea. In 1971, journalists Villy Bergström and Kurt Wickman and photographer Arne Hjort were naive enough to believe that they would be meeting with Kim Il-sung, and would be able to wander freely in Pyongyang and converse with workers and farmers. Instead, they were taken along a prescribed path of drawn-out visits to cult sites dedicated to Kim Il-sung and his dynasty, as well as the Korean Revolution Museum, exemplary daycare centres, and ironworks.

Ironworks aren't on our itinerary, but generally speaking, the trip the journalists took and ours match up: the obligatory monuments in Pyongyang, Kaesong, and Panmunjom, for example. Going by other travel accounts, not much has changed — the same routes and the same rhetoric for the past forty years.

Bergström, Wickman, and Hjort published an account of their journey called *Pictures from North Korea (Bilder från Nordkorea)*. At the time, the book was criticized for taking too hard a stance against North Korea, but in later years it was held up as a grotesque whitewashing of a horrific dictatorship.

Pictures from North Korea isn't at all the whitewashing that critics make it out to be. Rather, it unfolds as an ironic reportage on the cult of personality around Kim Il-sung and his family, which had already reached monumental proportions by 1971. Sure, there's a desire among the three leftists to see the positive in the North Korean model, but it is worth noting that the book was written before the catastrophic famine, in a period when South Korea was a severe military dictatorship and North Korean industry was operating at full throttle. And though the three travellers wanted to find a utopia on the other side of the earth, a place where socialism had succeeded, they were soon driven to madness by their guides' evasion tactics and the droning speeches about Kim Il-sung's achievements.

Bergström wrote about their visit to Kim Il-sung

University in Pyongyang. (The same stop was on our itinerary, but for some reason it was cancelled.) He and his friends had made a special request to meet professors of economics in order to discuss the North Korean economy. But the professors held their tongues, and instead the dean took their guests to the so-called "animal room," where jars of fish, and stuffed foxes, wolves, and bears were on display. Each specimen had been caught and killed by Kim Il-sung himself, who had then sent them to the university so that the students could study these rare examples of Korean fauna. The dean then explained that brave comrade Kim Il-sung had also shot an enormous tiger, "the largest tiger ever to be brought down in Korea." The leader's hunting rifles and dog were proudly displayed, together with the taxidermied animal.

Bergström, who was a hunter, noticed that the shotgun was a twelve-calibre, double-barrelled Sauer & Sohn from East Germany, "one that's fit for pheasant and hare, possibly a deer at an extremely close range." The hunting dog turned out to be "an Irish Setter, a so-called pointer, known for its ability to point to partridges, pheasants and grouse."

Later, Bergström learned the history of the hunting dog from some Finnish friends. In the 1950s, the pro-Communist Australian war correspondent Wilfred Burchett had been in the demilitarized zone of Panmunjom, reporting on the ceasefire negotiations between the North and South. There, the journalist came across a wretched mutt. He adopted the dog, caring for it until it recovered and in time became a handsome hound. Then one day the dog disappeared, never to return again.

Burchett returned to North Korea in the mid-1960s, as a guest at an international congress of journalists in Pyongyang. Like Bergström and his friends, he was taken on the obligatory guided tour of Kim Il-sung University. When Burchett entered the animal room, he caught sight of the hunting dog that was displayed next to the tiger. He exclaimed: "Oh, there's Prince!"

*   *   *

WE ARE STANDING in a forest in front of a log cabin that is said to be the birthplace of Kim Jong-il. On the way to the cabin we passed a spring where Andrei took a water sample. A uniformed guide has been called over. She moves with choreographed revolutionary gestures — probably inspired by movies and parades — lengthening her neck and raising her arm ninety degrees, her palm flat and straight. With a strained, declamatory voice she recounts the story of how Kim Il-sung came up with the guerilla warfare strategy against the Japanese army.

THE OFFICIAL NORTH Korean praise of Kim Il-sung is similar to how the first leader of unified China, the Emperor of Qin, was addressed by his people: "the First," "radiant," and "demi-god." If you want a more realistic biographical description, you have to look beyond North Korea. American author and journalist Bradley K. Martin's authoritative biography *Under the Loving Care of the Fatherly Leader* describes how Kim Il-sung was born outside Pyongyang in 1912, but was primarily raised in Manchuria. Early on, he became involved in the Young Communist League and was imprisoned as a teenager for anti-Japanese activities. When he was in his twenties, he joined the resistance movement in Manchuria, which was supported by the Soviet Union. In the Chinese army in the 1930s, he led a squadron of 200 men that raided a town occupied by the Japanese. It was also in this decade that he took the name Kim Il-sung, meaning "become the sun." In 1942 — the official year that Kim Jong-suk (Kim Il-sung's first wife, who was also a guerilla soldier) gave birth to Kim Jong-il — the family was living in a training camp in the village of Vyatskoye, north of Khabarovsk in the Soviet Union.

The USSR declared war on Japan in 1945, and the Red Army rolled into Pyongyang on August 15 with little resistance. One week later, Kim Il-sung arrived from Moscow. That same year, at the Potsdam Conference, the Korean question didn't make it onto the agenda. But a few weeks after the conference, Harry S. Truman suddenly made a suggestion to Joseph Stalin: Korea should be divided at the 38th parallel, because that was just about the middle of the peninsula. Truman hadn't been prepared for Japan's quick capitulation and was now worried that the Red Army would continue its march South. Surprisingly, Stalin accepted the suggestion of a divided protectorate in which the Soviet Union would take responsibility for North Korea and the United States for the South for a period of five years.

In 1948, power in the South was turned over to Rhee Syng-man, South Korea's first president, and one year later the U.S. Army began withdrawing troops from the region.

That same year, the Soviet Army also withdrew from North Korea, and Kim Il-sung founded the Democratic People's Republic of Korea and was rechristened "the Great Leader." Lavrentiy Beria, the marshal of the Soviet Union, had advised Stalin that Kim Il-sung would be a suitable puppet in Pyongyang. But they underestimated him. In a short period of time, Kim Il-sung built up the Korean People's Army around a core group of former guerilla soldiers. The Soviets contributed heavy artillery and industrial support as an investment in their political control.

Both leaders considered themselves the self-evident and rightful leaders of the entire Korean peninsula. Kim Il-sung wanted to liberate the South, and when his troops crossed the border on June 25, 1950, thereby signalling the start of the Korean War, the success of the North seemed imminent. In three days, the North Korean army took Seoul, and then continued south. By August, they had taken the entire country with the exception of a tiny point far down in the south. The United Nations agreed that the civil war should be considered an act of aggression by the North, and in September troops bearing the UN flag arrived in the city of Incheon, just outside Seoul. This aspect of the Korean War — that there were a number of nations fighting alongside the Americans in Korea — has notably fallen into oblivion. Even though the United States orchestrated the war, Ethiopian, Turkish, Canadian, Australian, and Colombian soldiers fought alongside them, and countries such as Sweden and Norway ran field hospitals, manned by the Red Cross and overseen by the United Nations.

General Douglas MacArthur, the commander of the UN forces, thought that intervening in Korean affairs would be smooth and simple, but the North Koreans were supported by China, and Mao's guerilla soldiers had been hardened by decades of unending war. They protected China's borders at any cost and were successful in pushing the UN troops back.

Over the course of the three years of war, the regime in Seoul changed four times, and the border continually shifted, extending and contracting until it was finally locked back in place at the 38th parallel, where it remains today. Both countries were devastated by the war, particularly the North. The American air force dropped up to 800 tons of bombs each day on North Korean cities. At a critical point, MacArthur requested the use of atomic bombs against China, but he was denied by Truman. Peace was never declared, only a ceasefire that took effect on July 27, 1953, which is still in place today.

IN THE 1950S, Kim Il-sung wrapped an iron fist around the North Korean government. Supported by the army and the secret service, and with a heavy dose of strategic thinking, he managed to eliminate his rivals for power and established the ultra-patriotic cult of personality as a tool to unify the people.

During the 1960s, Kim Il-sung sent his troops on a number of guerilla raids in South Korea, but over the following decades he rarely left the country. Instead, he devoted himself to on-the-spot guidance — that is, like a Renaissance-era prince he travelled the land and imparted wisdom on issues large and small. Soon all inventions, all research, all agricultural methods, and many medical treatments and artistic expressions would in principle be attributed to Kim Il-sung's personal engagement and general brilliance, just as in times past all decrees, laws, and rules of conduct bore the emperor's seal. To live the ideal, virtuous life was to live as Kim Il-sung advocated. The vestiges of his visits were cared for like sacred relics: the chairs he sat on were placed on pedestals; the routes he took to factories were recreated in models with blinking lamps showing the way. It was at this time that the tender image of Kim Il-sung emerged: a hard-working parent who came home from work and embraced all of his children.

In 1972 Kim Il-sung took the title of president, but by that time his son Kim Jong-il had most likely taken over many of his duties. Kim Il-sung had fathered a total of nine children, three of whom were illegitimate. One of them drowned at the age of five while playing with his brother Kim Jong-il; in 1949, a daughter died at birth along with her mother. Each child, even the illegitimate ones, was given a high-ranking position within the government, but none could compete with Kim Jong-il for power.

In 1980, the political situation in South Korea was in crisis. President Park Chung-hee had been assassinated in late 1979, leaving the country in a state of political instability. Shortly after, General Chun Doo-hwan took control of the government through a military *coup d'état*. Students and professors led nationwide pro-democratization movements in response. In May 1980, a large uprising in the city of Gwangju was brutally quashed by armed soldiers. The peaceful demonstrations against President Chun Doo-hwan incited the military to react with sadistic violence against the young and the old, resulting in more than 200 civilian casualties. The massacre in Gwangju is still the deepest wound in the history of the nation.

In spite of the impressive economic growth over the past decade, the violence, along with government corruption and various financial scandals, caused the rest of the world to look upon the country with distrust. Now it was feared that civil war would break out in South Korea. In response, North Korea mobilized their troops along the border. If the chaos continued, the troops would only have to march southward. But the situation in the South stabilized, while the economy in the North weakened.

ON MONDAY NOVEMBER 17, 1986, the South Korean government announced that Kim Il-sung had been assassinated while on a train. The information is said to have come from the North Korean loudspeakers that had been set up near the demilitarized zone to spread propaganda to the South. Flags waving at half mast had also been spotted, and doleful music could heard playing in the North. The reaction in the South was strong and chaos ensued. Kyodo News, the Japanese news agency, reported that the Workers' Party of North Korea had sent a message to Vietnam's Communist Party that Kim Il-sung had been assassinated. Contradictory reports from North Korea followed, but the South Koreans insisted that something had happened, possibly a military coup. It was later speculated that Kim Il-sung's doppelganger had been murdered.

It would be another eight years until Kim Il-sung actually passed away. By the time Kim Jong-il took power in 1994, the situation in the country was catastrophic. Goods had not come in from Moscow for several years; manufacturing had severely diminished; the electrical grid was on the verge of collapse; and the country was completely isolated from the rest of the world. Since 1992, the people had been encouraged to eat two rather than three meals a day. For the four years following Kim Il-sung's death, the country was paralyzed by mourning rituals, starvation, bad harvests, and inaction around the changeover of the throne. Kim Jong-il had isolated himself in his palace, ordering the building of monuments to his father and blaming the Americans — "the American imperialist pigs," as he often called them — for the country's hardships. Infrastructure broke down, the rationing system stopped working, and people were desperately searching for ways to survive.

As democracy broke through in South Korea at the start of the 1990s, North Korea began to slip into the abyss. When Kim Dae-jung — a dissident who had been severely mistreated by the secret service and imprisoned with a death sentence hanging over him — was elected as president in 1997, it was an incredible moment. The Sunshine Policy, which drastically altered South Korea's policy toward the North by offering financial, food, and developmental aid for the first time since the division of the two countries, marked a period of détente and culminated in an historic summit meeting with Kim Jong-il in Pyongyang. For opening up a dialogue with the North Korean enemy, Kim Dae-jung was awarded the Nobel Peace Prize in 2000.

AS HEAD OF state during the 2000s, Kim Jong-il took to the world stage, shaking hands with various other heads of state and ministers: Kim Dae-jung, U.S. Secretary of State Madeleine Albright, Russian President Vladimir Putin, Japanese Prime Minister Junichiro Koizumi, and in the spring of 2001, Swedish Prime Minister Göran Persson, who was then president of the European Council. Following his meeting with Kim Jong-il, Persson said in an interview on Sweden's SVT channel: "If that was indeed Kim Jong-il who we met, I should say. I wouldn't know, but we assume it was. Still, you can't ever rule anything out."

After September 10, 2003, Kim Jong-il disappeared. He wasn't seen in public for forty-two days. When he met Prime Minister Koizumi again in 2004, the meeting lasted only ninety minutes. Toshimitsu Shigemura, a professor at Waseda University in Tokyo who is considered an expert on North Korea, claimed that Kim Jong-il had died of diabetes and had been replaced by a doppelganger. This would explain the brief meeting with Koizumi — the doppelganger didn't want to risk giving himself away. Professor Shigemura tried to support his theory by showing photos of Kim Jong-il where it appeared that he had grown nearly an inch taller. He also referred to pictures in which the leader's four ever-present, highly ranked military men were, according to the professor, ferrying the doppelganger around like a puppet.

These four men were actually the ones who were in power, said Shigemura.

If this speculative theory was correct, it was the doppelganger who was now emaciated and ageing. Like the warlord in Akira Kurosawa's *Kagemusha*, the doppelganger had inhabited his role as leader so fully that he had become the leader. In Kurosawa's film, as the illusion takes shape the environment around the stand-in warlord responds accordingly: family, servants, and subjects play along. The power of the performance finally causes him to lose his ability to differentiate between reality and theatre. Out of hubris, the doppelganger tries to ride the warlord's horse but is thrown off. Even a powerful illusion has its limits.

*   *   *

WE ARE STARING incredulously at the log cabin on the slopes of Mount Baekdu, where the guide claims that Kim Jong-il was born. The cabin is at most twenty years old.

When we walk back to the bus, we pass trees with protective coverings, placed there to preserve the revolutionary scrawls that Kim Il-sung is supposed to have carved into the trunks for posterity. These are the so-called "slogan trees," a new form of cult site created in the 1980s, when revolutionary notes written in Kim Il-sung's hand were suddenly discovered. It was reported in *Rodong Sinmun* that in October 2002, seventeen firemen died trying to protect a slogan tree with their bodies. Found in their charred hands were the pins that feature Kim Il-sung's portrait, badges that all

North Koreans wear on their chests. They held on to them until the end.

* * *

CULT SITES IN North Korea barely conceal that they are mere façades. The act of naming and the stories are more important then the materializations. In the cinematic arts, on the other hand, façades are in service of the illusion. In a film, you can't walk around a log cabin and identify its obvious flaws. In the darkness of a movie theatre, you don't have a body — you are two eyes being drawn into the world of the story without resistance.

Going to the movies is not a voluntary activity in North Korea — it's the duty of every citizen. In the country's annual official report on film, the rules are laid out together with statistics on screenings. It is logical that a leader like Kim Jong-il, who devotes so much of his energy to myth-building, would invest heavily in filmmaking as a tool to shape citizens. But his interest isn't only out of necessity; one realizes it is also the leader's personal passion and desire.

Even Kim Il-sung was a dedicated film buff. The party's elite could watch any film they liked, even if it had been made by the enemy. In isolation, they could enjoy Shin Sang-ok's melodramas. As early as 1958 Kim Il-sung had said: "The cinema should have great appeal and move ahead of the realities." He saw how Stalin's image had radically changed over time in the Soviet Union and how after his death Mao was devalued in China. With the help of cinema, Kim Il-sung felt he could secure his posthumous radiance. By appointing his cinephile son as his successor, the great opera, the work of art that was his life, would be passed down through film. Kim Jong-il was a patron, a producer of something that could be refashioned and replayed for all eternity.

A FEW YEARS before the kidnapping of Choi Eun-hee and Shin Sang-ok, Kim Jong-il wrote a book about film called *On the Art of the Cinema*. It was here that Kim Jong-il established that art, literature, and film should be Juche-focused. It's not easy to parse what this means. Kim Jong-il discusses everything from the script to the skill of the cinematographer, make-up artist, editor, and scenographer, as well as the importance of music and engaged acting, but the advice consists mainly of general and meaningless statements: "One must aim high in creation," "Make-up is a noble art," "The best words are filled with meaning and are easy to understand," "Each scene must be dramatic," "Begin on a small scale and end grandly," and on and on.

Kim Jong-il says that an actor's interpretation of a character must be based on his own experiences and empathy. At first this sentiment may seem like a crack in the wall of ideological bunkum — putting the actor in a position where he must fully inhabit his enemy. He uses the example of an actor who is supposed to play a Japanese policeman — that is, a bad guy — and tries to imagine the character's backstory. But, according to Kim Jong-il, this is the wrong approach: a depiction of the enemy must emerge from the feeling of genuine hate—a hate that is as large as the love for your own people and the working class.

ACCORDING TO HIS official biography, Kim Jong-il displayed his understanding of film as a seven-year-old when he observed that the snow falling in a movie looked like cotton balls. It is also said that over the course of his life he took part in the production of 800 feature-length films, 400 children's films, and 1,000 documentaries. And his personal archive is thought to include more than 15,000 titles, exclusively in 35mm prints.

A 2005 article in *Film International* describes how North Korean diplomats in Berlin helped stock Kim Jong-il's film archive. Mr. U Kun-chol—the secretary of economic affairs at the Office for the Protection of the Interests of the Democratic People's Republic of Korea, which had been housed in the North Korean embassy's concrete colossus in East Berlin before the wall fell—went trundling along to offices of the local film distributors. He carried with him a long list of movies that he wanted to have transferred to 35mm. He was given the cold shoulder everywhere he went.

U Kun-chol didn't give in. He sought out contacts in the alternative Berlin film scene, and in 2000 Johannes Schönherr, a trash-movie collector and pornographer well known in underground circles, became his closest collaborator.

With the help of an interpreter, Mr. U called Schönherr almost every day. Initially, he was in acute need of a fifteen-part film series about the Yakuza wives, as well as a German TV movie about the life of Catherine the Great. This was the first in a long line of requests for films about European royalty, and he was prepared to pay any price.

Mr. U would never admit that these films were going to be sent to Kim Jong-il. Instead, he insisted that the staff at his office in Berlin was made up of devoted connoisseurs of cinema and no less than 35mm prints would do. When Schönherr explained there was no soundtrack for the 35mm version of *Catherine the Great*, and that it would cost tens of thousands of dollars to make a screening copy, Mr U would not be deterred by such trivialities.

"No problem, we'll pay," he said. "Don't give up, make sure to get a hold of that film."

Also high up on the wish list was the 2000 South Korean blockbuster *Shiri* by Kang Je-gyu. The film is inspired by the true story of the North Korean agent Kim Hyon-hui, who was trained from the age of eighteen as part of a plot to sabotage South Korea. In 1987, she and a fellow agent placed a bomb on a South Korean passenger plane that was flying from Abu Dhabi to Seoul. The plane exploded and all the passengers died. The order was said to have come directly from Kim Jong-il with the aim of discrediting South Korea's security measures in advance of the 1988 Olympics in Seoul.

In *Shiri*, the stunning female protagonist goes through a training program similar to that of the real agent, Kim Hyon-hui, including learning a deadly karate chop, target practice, and extreme physical exercises. She is sent to Seoul to assassinate various political dignitaries and military bigwigs. She is an angel of death wearing blood-red lipstick and a trench coat, and her long-distance shots to the head are clinically precise. The purpose of the attack is to create chaos that will pave the way for a reunification of North and South, thus creating a new Great Korean Empire.

For Kim Jong-il, obtaining a copy of *Shiri* must have been the final, vital link in a chain of events that he himself had initiated. He'd ordered an attack, engaging the help of a beautiful agent, and the event had inspired a lavish feature film with a juicy plot that he now could sit back and enjoy with a snifter of cognac. This is the kind of thing that makes a leader feel powerful: your life has a purpose and your actions make such an impact that they are staged and forever mythologized.

KIM JONG-IL WAS eager to discuss film with Choi Eun-hee. He couldn't stress enough the importance of cinema as a conduit for national fellowship. Madame had free access to both the film archive and Kim's private screening room. The archive was generally only accessible to the ruling family, but in a way, Kim Jong-il considered her part of the family. He seemed to have forgotten that she was connected to them by force.

Certain films in the archive were used to instruct North Korean filmmakers, and one of these was Shin Sang-ok's *Evergreen Tree*, which ironically was the same film that General Park considered South Korea's national epic. Madame could watch what she liked, but she was encouraged to study propaganda documentaries about North Korean history and Russian films set during the revolution. One of the films Madame was ordered to see was called *This Shouldn't Exist*, which showed poverty, crime, and "bad behaviour" among North Koreans. This cautionary tale was intended to help prevent people from behaving inappropriately, but it gave a glimpse of life beyond the propaganda.

After a while, Madame Choi could express her opinions quite openly to Kim Jong-il. She explained to him that she found the film version of Kim Il-sung's opera *Sea of Blood* poorly produced and clumsily costumed. She asserted that revolution wasn't the only theme in the film; love was too, for example.

On one of these occasions, Kim Jong-il cryptically replied: "We'll resolve this when director Shin arrives."

*   *   *

THE BUS TAKES us back to Samjiyon Airport, and the final forty kilometres are driven on the perfectly straight military roads that the Japanese built in 1939. Another military airplane — a somewhat newer model than the one that brought us here — is parked on the runway in the forest clearing. When we climb on board, one of the Värmlanders says: "It smells like manure. It's just like home."

The stewardesses are wearing Air Koryo uniforms and serve us each one glass of beer during the flight back to Pyongyang. We get used to the manure smell. Ms. Kim takes care of the matsutake mushrooms that have been with us since the visit to Mount Chilbo. She holds the basket on her lap; white plastic bands with red text have been wrapped around their stalks.

94

Also on the plane is a man in an air force uniform. He takes the seat farthest back in the plane, between two stewardesses. He jokes loudly with the two women and has a hard time keeping his hands to himself. Then he moves to sit down next to us and shows us a small photo album of his family. He lives in a lovely apartment. His wife is wearing a pink blouse and a pearl necklace in the pictures, and his son is about ten and has a drum kit. With a look of contentment he points to the photo of his son and says: "Fat."

IF YOU DON'T count the parking lot outside the Yanggakdo Hotel, we have yet to set foot on the streets of Pyongyang. During the bus ride from the airport, Mr. Song tells us that now, finally, we'll be going out into the city to look at some important sites.

"But remember," he says. "Never stray from the group. Ask if you want to take pictures."

It's late in the afternoon when we roll into Pyongyang. We stop near the Monument to Party Founding. The group rushes off the bus and scatters in all directions. Mr. Song and Ms. Kim try to call Elias and Oksana back, but they are already on their way down into the subway.

Mr. Song breaks into a sweat but maintains his composure. After rounding us all up, he shepherds us to the monument. The view is panoramic: you can see the Mangyongdae Children's Palace, one of Pyongyang's largest theatres, and the Taedong River farther off. A row of schoolchildren in red Youth Corps uniforms march past; the line seems never-ending. An overcrowded tram passes by, so crammed that people are clinging on to the back and sides.

"No pictures!" Mr. Song yells.

*   *   *

EN ROUTE TO the Rungrado 1st of May Stadium, we pass the Potonggang Hotel, owned by Pastor Moon Sun-myung. It's remarkable that Moon, who is an incredibly wealthy cult leader, has allied himself with the powers in North Korea. The pastor is from the North, but was put in a work camp in 1948 for evangelizing. In 1950, during the Korean War, he was released from the camp when its guards fled as UN troops advanced.

In South Korea, Moon laid the foundation of his religious movement with a combination of charismatic authority, business sense, and self-mythologization. Within the Unification Church, as his movement is called, he was later given the status of Resurrected Jesus. The cult focused its recruitment on young people, often naive students who were then put under great strain with a combination of hard work, little sleep, and surveillance. In 1971 the enterprise moved to the United States, where he managed to build up a financial empire that now donates large sums of money to American right-wing organizations. Moon founded the *Washington Times* in 1982, which became a soapbox for extreme right-wing Republicans. It was also one of the few newspapers to be granted a long interview with Kim Il-sung. In 1992, the entire staff was flown to Pyongyang to produce the issue in honour of the leader's eightieth birthday. The interview was nothing more than an obsequious display for Kim's benefit.

Pastor Moon managed to grow close to Kim Il-sung and became good friends with those who held high positions within the regime. Large financial transactions from the church's business dealings had laid the foundation.

There seems to be a strong resonance between Moon's ruling strategy and that of the Kim clan — notably Moon's mass weddings and North Korea's mass events, but most of all the cult of personality and the deification of an individual — and the two leaders also have similar views on their disciples' moral obligations.

In 2004, Moon appeared at an awards dinner at the Dirksen Senate Office Building in Washington, D.C. — an event that he and his wife, wearing crowns and burgundy robes, turned into a coronation ceremony. By then he had already established intimate contact with Kim Jong-il, who had taken over his father's business alliances and friendships. With this alignment of the heavenly bodies of the Moon King and the Sun King, the Unification Church's future in North Korea was secured. Hotel Potonggang is still the only sign of Moon in the city, but the pastor has been given a ninety-nine-year lease on the village of his birth, where he is planning a great expansion: establishing the holy city of the Unification Church.

* * *

FROM A DISTANCE, the Rungrado 1st of May Stadium looks like a giant parachute that has landed in the Taedong River and hardened into concrete. With a capacity of 150,000, this is the world's largest arena. A war is being waged here — not with weapons, but with theatre. The enemy is Hollywood, and to triumph over Hollywood the "world's greatest performance," as the program states, must be created. And we are going to bear witness to it.

The Grand Mass Gymnastics and Artistic Performance Arirang, as it is called, is performed every year with different themes. This year, the sixtieth anniversary of the founding of North Korea, the theme is "Prosper Ye Motherland." As Song Sok-hwang, the director of the Mass Games, said in an interview: "The U.S. imperialists are trying to stifle us. They create a negative image of North Korea. I hope Arirang helps to counter that."

"Arirang" is a 600-year-old Korean folk song that is essentially a woman's lament over the loss of a lover and her hope of seeing him again. During the performance, the song is used as a metaphor for the longing to be reunited with the South; in other contexts and depending on the political situation, it has taken on completely different meanings. During colonial times *Arirang* (1926) was made into a silent movie and it is considered to be the first film to articulate Korean nationalism. In time, it became a national treasure. After Korea's liberation from Japan, the only copy in existence disappeared. Later, a Japanese collector with 50,000 films in his archive claimed that it was in his possession. Kim Jong-il was prepared to pay any price for *Arirang*, but the man replied that he would dispose of the copy only by order of the Japanese emperor.

THE ROOF OF the stadium is open, and we see how swiftly darkness falls and how the stars in the sky emerge. The seats on the opposite side fill quickly, with row after row of young boys in white shirts. Their heads look like black balls rolling along the rows of benches. A wondrous logistical feat has them in their seats in ten minutes. Each of them holds a 170-page catalogue of coloured paper. Thirty thousand school-boys take their places as part of this giant, living screen, where each individual represents one pixel.

Ari and Trond are buzzing with anticipation. They stand and start waving a North Korean flag. Our ever-present videographer turns his camera on them: he can't miss this.

The stands fill up with people wearing the brown Home Guard uniforms. Soon, a great mass of people have arrived. Their uniformity makes us think of soccer fans; but unlike soccer fans with their waving and shouting, this group is silent.

They've put us Westerners together in a middle section. There are probably 200 of us here. A group of Germans are mounting telescopic lenses on tripods, breathless with anticipation. One of them wears a black dress and heavy chrome chains around his neck. Another wears shiny leather pants; the back of his head is shaved but he sports long, bleached New Wave–style bangs at the front.

The children on the other side of the stadium start to stamp their feet in unison. Together, they let out a blood-curdling howl that swells over the stands in a wave of sound, creating what feels like the world's largest live surround-sound system.

Ten thousand girl-gymnasts in red, yellow, and blue costumes spill out onto the grass field and form groups. With their coloured papers, the schoolchildren in the stands create alternating horizontal and vertical fields of colour. At every transition, they let out a wave of screams that sets an uneasy atmosphere in the stadium. After having flipped through the colour catalogue like an old-fashioned television running through test images, they finally seem to "get reception." The words "60 years of the motherland," flanked by a bouquet of flowers with long, graceful garlands, materializes against a light-blue background. Next up is a panoramic image of Mount Baekdu shrouded in mist. Heaven Lake shifts between turquoise and green, and the slopes of the mountain are the colour of the gloaming. On the field, the gymnasts stand in formation, emulating a hundred-metre-long North Korean flag spread out on the ground. It moves as if blown by a gentle wind.

We watch the performance breathlessly. We have a hard time making sense of our impressions and understanding what it is that we are seeing. This is perhaps the most remarkable visual experience we have ever witnessed. The images created on the stands opposite act as a backdrop to the abundance of events on the grassy field. Laser projections and layers of animation accentuate the details on the schoolchildren's pictures. Strings of tens of thousands of small lamps create intricate patterns against the night sky. Sequences of moving images are projected onto the sheets of paper that the children are holding. There are melo-dramatic scenes of loss, separation, and reunion. Arms reach for each other and are torn apart. People weep from sorrow and happiness. An epic drama is played out using interludes of musicals, gymnastic routines, acrobatics, and parades. At one point, the schoolchildren create the image of two guns, a symbol of the fight against the Japanese. At another point, the symbol for an atom.

Actors of all ages participate in the show. A segment with small children doing a dance routine dressed as eggs tran-sitions to a scene depicting the power of factories and the machinery of war. Cuteness is mixed with familiar Com-munist iconography: clenched fists, farm machinery, water-driven power plants, and smiling workers arm in arm with doctors and soldiers. The performance is like a giant pop-up book chronicling North Korea's sixty years of suffering and progress. But most of all it is asserting unity, which is created by the synchronized movements of the masses. A hundred thousand people are performing tonight. How many more are involved in the transport, catering, costumes, scenog-raphy, music, medical care, security, and technical support? A significant portion of Pyongyang's population must be involved, on or off stage. Anyone who's not involved and who is able-bodied is in the audience.

We have now reached the grand finale. The face of Kim Jong-il, the Sun King, appears. Radiant yellow gradually transitions into a deep red hue. Kim Jong-il's theories from his 1994 book about Juche, *Socialism Is a Science*, are given an overwhelming representation in the displays of synchronization in the Arirang show. His corporeal analogies are repeated in communication, news articles, decrees, and pedagogy. The Great Leader is the brain that plots, plans, and commands. The party is the nervous system that receives the leader's signals and sends them on to the people who make up the flesh, tendons, and muscles — the parts of the body that perform the work.

THE STANDS EMPTY out, and we notice that one of the Germans has collapsed. He has vomited and is now lying on his side on a bench. A North Korean guide wipes his forehead.

We are also shaken up. We understand that we have just met the Monster. It's the same monster you see in the frontispiece of Thomas Hobbes's *Leviathan*, a historic work of political philosophy published in 1651. Hobbes used a monster metaphor to illustrate how a leader stands above his people. When the Leviathan was constructed, all the citizens promised to obey the sovereign leader. The sovereign, on the other hand, promised nothing. He was above promises, and the rules that applied to the citizenry could not be applied to him. His supreme position was meant to protect the state from civil war and fratricide.

Hobbes's frontispiece depicts the upper body of a gigantic person with a crown, staff, and sword. The creature's body is made up of a mass of individuals, but the face is the leader's face. This image articulates the leader's relationship to the state and its subjects, as Kim Jong-il speaks of the Juche body. The way the Leviathan fuses the leader and the people is mirrored by the schoolchildren in the stadium, acting as pixels in the image of Kim Jong-il. But in the engraving we're not allowed to see the lower half of the body. We can only imagine what's hiding beneath the surface: the monster's scaly tail.

THE HAWAIIAN
GOOD LUCK SIGN

IN 1548, THE Holy Roman Emperor Charles V visited the atelier of the Italian painter Titian to see how his portrait was progressing. The picture had been commissioned to commemorate the emperor's victory over the Protestant princes in the Battle of Mühlberg on April 24, 1547. When Titian dropped his brush on the floor, the emperor stooped down and picked it up. It was a pivotal moment: for the first time, a Renaissance emperor was waiting on an artist.

The Hungarian art historian Arnold Hauser uses this image of the emperor on bent knee to articulate a paradigm shift: the artist no longer knelt down before the patron; the patron praised the artist. It's no longer the artist who praises the patron, the patron praises the artist. From here on patrons were themselves exalted by exalting the artists.

In the late 1500s, when Michelangelo was at the height of his fame, he transcended even this elevated status. Whereas Titian had social aspirations, Michelangelo was above earthly titles. "He says he is simply Michelangelo Buonarroti, no more, no less," Hauser writes. He was the first "modern, lonely, demonically impelled artist," and spoke of being possessed by a vision and having a responsibility to his talent. He saw a superhuman power in his creative abilities.

Michelangelo did not bask in the power of the prince; rather, he despised the prince. As Hauser noted: "The world whose glory it was his task to proclaim, now proclaims his glory; the cult of which he was the instrument now applies to him; the state of divine favor is now transferred from his patrons and protectors to himself."

LONG BEFORE, IN the old high cultures of antiquity, this reciprocal relationship between art and power was unimaginable. In ancient Greece, playing out of tune was punishable by death. In China, the lengths of the flutes were altered when a new emperor ascended the throne. The sound-making material had to have the same resonance as the person in power. Power was divine and dissonance was a crime against the gods.

But the idea of the free artist with a certain sparkle to his star lives on in the twenty-first century, while the prince, in popular imagination, has been relegated to the past. Even the modern European royal dynasties, with their ceremonial displays of authority, have hardly any actual power. Royal sovereignty has been transferred to the oligarchs and global capitalists. And the role of the dictator seems to have been written off, or written into history, judging by the volumes of biographies hitting the market about leaders such as Hitler, Stalin, Pol Pot, and Mao, all of whom had a hand in the horrific events that shaped the twentieth century.

In the modern network-economy and in globalization, power is thought of as liquid, immaterial, intangible, and incorporeal. Within this framework, the dictator can seem like an anachronistic character. But in some of the former Soviet republics, leaders cling to the luxury and eccentricities associated with German medieval princes and certain Renaissance royal families. Kalmykia, an autonomous republic in Russia, has been governed by the authoritarian leader known as the "King of Chess," Kirsan Ilyumzhinov. Ilyumzhinov has spent a substantial part of the impoverished nation's budget on soccer and chess; he even built an entire neighbourhood within the borders of the capital, Elista, devoted to chess. The King of Chess often sought the counsel of Vanga, a Bulgarian psychic, and has claimed that in September 1997 he was abducted by aliens. The title of his autobiography is *The President's Crown of Thorns*.

Meanwhile Saparmurat Niyazov, the former president of Turkmenistan, had a sculpture of himself built on top of a seventy-five-metre tower—a shining gold opus that rotates a full 360 degrees over the course of each day so that it is always facing the sun. While Niyazov was in power, every Turkmen citizen, young or old, had to spend one day a week studying his book *Ruhnama* (*The Book of the Soul*), a religious text on which he conferred the same status as the Koran. You couldn't even take your driving test if you didn't know your *Ruhnama*. Niyazov also changed the names of certain days of the week and certain months so that they were named after members of his family. When the dictator died in 2006, he was replaced by Gurbanguly Berdymuchamedov, a man who could have been his doppelganger. Dissidents who had nurtured a sliver of hope that the new regime would bring change were shocked to see Niyazov "resurrected," embodied by Berdymuchamedov. International news bureaus confused pictures of the deceased with those of his double.

As for Vladimir Putin—who has perhaps been most successful in camouflaging his near-total power, even if the camouflage has gradually become more and more transparent—he has styled himself as an action figure, assembling various *mise en scènes* of his vision of a powerful man: posing bare-chested in sable fur with tiger cubs, in camouflage gear, in a judo uniform, and in other suitably imposing outfits. Above all, he has demonstrated how all these roles can be embodied by one and the same person.

OUR MODERN-DAY PRINCE Kim Jong-il persists in his fragile existence. With the ability of the media and the Internet to instantly disseminate information and images, we have never been more aware of the physical bodies of our leaders as we are now. A leader's metabolism can be directly connected to the global economy. When George H. W. Bush vomited in the lap of Prime Minister Kiichi Miyazawa on January 8, 1992, during a state visit to Japan, markets around the world slumped. The media and global capitalism have created a capillary system of feedback between individual bodies and various global entities, and every action could cause biomedical chain reactions: poisoning, hallucination, leakage, and finding the antidote. Perhaps this is the most concrete definition of biopolitics. When on August 14, 1945, the Japanese emperor Hirohito announced on the radio that Japan had surrendered to the Allied powers, there was a national outcry. The emperor was considered divine, a being from whom you averted your eyes. So his admission of Japan's defeat, in which he spoke directly to his subjects for the first time during his reign, was doubly shocking. The divine had become corporeal, and the unthinkable had been acknowledged.

IN THE PAST, the distinction between a leader's symbolic and physical existence was made clear through a long series of ceremonies, rituals, and incantations. German historian Ernst Kantorowicz describes these rituals in *The King's Two Bodies* (1957). When a king died, a set of transitional ceremonies was set in motion in order to articulate the physical body's departure from the political body. In a way, this was to prevent unease around succession. "The king is dead. Long live the king!" is the classic formulation, which summarizes this need for order and continuity. Important documents, regalia, and ceremonial clothing would be displayed during a procession, and these were then presented to the new king. The political, symbolic body lives on beyond death and is transferred to the new ruler.

Processions, which had once been displays of rank and power in Europe, are still enacted on a grand scale in North

Korea. All the objects and monuments that have been constructed to symbolize the emperor's every talent and duty are used to maximum effect. The oaths that were once held between the regent and his subjects are here in the form of education. The connection between the leader and the people takes shape in many ways: triumphal arches, giant mosaics, mass performances, parades, operas, and above all films—all the things that strengthen ties to the ruler and discipline his subjects.

In most parts of the world, these rituals have disappeared, which means that the leader's political body has merged with his physical one. This is a sensitive point: acute biopolitical crises emerge in societies and economies that rise and fall in accordance with their leader's well-being. A democratic society with parliamentary power strives to avoid such sensitive ties, but this is in vain if the media performs the paradoxical work of both iconifying and chastening the leader's body. Certain democratically elected heads of state don't need golden statues of themselves to adorn cities, nor countless colour portraits hung in post offices. The enormous media exposure they receive iconifies their image just as effectively. The frequent and repeated reproduction of an image in the media elevates the standing of the image's subject, who begins to radiate a unique aura.

Kim Jong-il has his own theory. In the "Theory of the Immortal Socio-Political Body," he uses bodily metaphors that echo Kantorowicz, contrasting the socio-political organism with the physical body. Political life is immortal and created by the socio-political body. Individuals die, but their souls will live on if they were devoted to their immortal leader in their lifetime.

LONG BEFORE KIM IL-SUNG's death, the North Koreans had begun to solve the problem of the king's two bodies with terminology. Kim Jong-il was referred to as "the Dear Leader," which implied succession. However, when death severed the father's physical body from his political body on July 8, 1994, there was a period of hesitancy. For three years, Kim Jong-il reigned as commander-in-chief. His father's death and the succession of power didn't seem to have been fully accepted by the people. The solution was to allow the departed Kim Il-sung to keep his post as president. Then there needn't be a transfer of power.

"The king is not dead! Long live the king!" became North Korea's answer to the old symbolics of succession.

*   *   *

OUR FIFTH DAY holds the promise of a grand tour of Pyongyang. This turns out to mean more monuments and memorials. The excursion begins at Kim Il-sung's birthplace, Mangyongdae, which is just over ten kilometres from Pyongyang; then the metro subway system; and after that the American spy ship the USS *Pueblo*, which was seized in January 1968 by the North Koreans.

At each of these sites, we wonder what we're actually looking at. The spinning wheel at Kim Il-sung's place of birth looks too perfect. The metro, deep down in the earth, is impressive with its candelabra and mosaics. Serious and silent people are neatly positioned on the escalators. Like all the other adults in Pyongyang, they wear a small pin bearing the Great Leader's portrait. In addition to uniforms, many men are wearing a North Korean version of the Mao suit, while others wear suit trousers and untucked shirts. Women wear blouses and skirts.

But the spinning wheel isn't at Mangyongdae by chance. As Kim Suk-young points out in *Illusive Utopia*, the spinning wheel has a central place in the mythology surrounding Kim Il-sung's mother, Gang Ban-seok. In the 1960s, she was held up as the country's feminine ideal. In *The Mother of Korea*, Gang's official biography, she is portrayed as a character taken straight from Greek mythology: "In the evening she used to spin together with her mother. She had learned to spin when she was a child, and now she could also weave. She did not just imitate others — watching them working she tried to work even better. Far from being satisfied with her results of today, she strove to achieve perfection tomorrow. She worked with such dexterity and skillfulness that all her movements seemed easy and graceful." The symbol of the spinning wheel links generations together — femininity and maternity are united in productivity. Countless stories are told about how Kim Il-sung's first wife adopted this skill, sewing uniforms for servicemen during the guerilla war as if her life depended on it.

Mr. Song offers no explanation as to why tourists are allowed to see only two of the seventeen metro stations. Are these the only stations worth looking at? According to one theory, the other fifteen don't exist, and all the well-dressed passengers are just extras riding back and forth between the two stops. But looking at the flood of people spilling from the subway car, it seems unlikely.

Defectors claim that there is an unofficial metro system with additional routes. This parallel system is for the upper echelons of society and connects the more important palaces with the airport. In this way, the wealthy can quickly be evacuated if war breaks out. The same defectors have also said that the metro is connected to an underground military system that includes shelters, a larger road where weapons and troops can be transported, and a giant bunker. The square in this bunker is said to be as large as Kim Il-sung Square and can hold 100,000 people.

We have been here only a few days, but we quickly understood that in North Korea the actual machinations of society are kept out of sight, underground, behind walls. The section of the population who are the richest live in Pyongyang. Until recently, all handicapped people were sent to the countryside so as not to sully the city's pristine image.

MR. SONG IS in high spirits as we are led around the USS *Pueblo*. The group behaves well. We look dutifully at the bullet holes that have been circled in pen — evidence of the machine-gun fire that the military directed at the pathetic American spies, who were already close to capitulation. The guide speaks mechanically about these heroic events.

All tourists are taken to the *Pueblo*. The ship is North Korea's most significant imperial trophy and a tool for propaganda. Photographs of the stooped American soldiers disembarking from the vessel have been put on stamps, and their surrender to North Korean soldiers is often recounted in literature and at school. As an example of this, B. R. Myers highlights "Snowstorm in Pyongyang," by one of North Korea's leading authors, Chon In-gwang. This short story contrasts the filth and depravity of the captives with the purity of the North Korean "child race." One of the American characters is homosexual, seen as the lowest of the low. The North Korean soldiers force the Americans to shower, but nothing can wash away their terrible odour. After a while, they refuse to cut the Americans' long, greasy hair.

Literature in North Korea is controlled completely by the state. In this way North Korea is unique: it is the only country where no dissident literature has ever surfaced. Which doesn't mean it doesn't exist—it just hasn't made it across the border.

THE EIGHTY-TWO AMERICAN captives from the USS *Pueblo* were ordered to be indoctrinated with the correct teachings, and they were photographed extensively. Guards rubbed hard-boiled eggs on the bags under their eyes so they would look as healthy as possible for the pictures.

During these photo shoots, the "Hawaiian Good Luck Sign" was created, a subversive phenomenon that our guide doesn't mention. In silent protest, prisoners gave the photographer the finger. But it was done subtly. In the photographs, you can see Americans scratching their foreheads, holding their fingers near the corner of their mouths, or leaning forward with their hands resting on the table, their middle fingers outstretched. After a while, the North Koreans started to see a pattern. They confronted the Americans, who innocently asked if their captors were familiar with the Hawaiian Good Luck Sign. The North Koreans were satisfied with this reply. The pictures were distributed to the global media and widely published. Coverage in an October 1968 issue of *Time* magazine mentioned the silent protest, and the North Koreans finally understood what the finger meant. The crew of the *Pueblo* suffered a "Hell Week" of torture and abuse.

* * *

UP ON DECK, Mr. Song takes the time to make a few jokes. He smiles, grabs a machine gun at the bow of the ship, and points it at us behind the guide's back. We smile back. The thing is, we're trying to get on Mr. Song's good side. We avoid critical questions and we obey his rules. We nod in agreement to his many statements: *Of course, Mr. Song; absolutely, Mr. Song; no problem, Mr. Song.* We're hoping to elicit favours — to be able to film and photograph as freely as possible — and moreover, to be taken into his confidence about how things really work here.

As we shuffle down the gangplank, Mr. Song laughs and says we look as humbled as the *Pueblo*'s crew when they were taken off the ship. We laugh with him; we're part of his gang now. We casually ask if it's true that there are only five acceptable haircuts for men. We read an article about it and saw a video from North Korean television posted on YouTube called "Let's trim our hair in accordance with the socialist lifestyle." In the video, people with unacceptable haircuts are secretly filmed on the street, and those who have crossed the line with wisps of hair hanging down the backs of their necks are stopped and questioned. Hairstyles like these are detrimental to human intelligence, the host proclaims. Long hair leaches nutrients, which leads to the brain being drained of energy. The ideal length is one and a half centimetres at the back of the head and five centimetres at the crown. Older men can have up to seven centimetres of hair to comb over a bald spot.

Mr. Song stiffens and looks worried. He wonders where we've gotten that information from. He asks if the article mentioned the punishment for having the wrong haircut.

LUNCH IS SERVED on a boat that sails slowly along the Taedong River. It's the best lunch yet. A large catfish is surrounded by kimchi and pickled radishes. We end up next to the Bromma boys, who tell us about their interest in travel — an interest that we soon learn leans toward shock tourism. They've come to North Korea via the Mongolian-Manchurian steppe and Beijing. After North Korea they are going on a guided tour of Afghanistan, where they'll travel in a convoy of armoured vehicles on the trail of known war sites. We tell them we've been to Iraq and one of them asks: "Do you have any tips?"

After the excellent meal, the group's energy is renewed and some of us start to take liberties again. Oksana has gone exploring along the river. Ms. Kim is on the verge of tears but the wind whisks away her words. Elias bombards Mr. Song with questions that he doesn't want to answer. When they finally manage to get the group back together, we are herded a couple hundred metres up to Kim Il-sung Square.

Mr. Song suddenly starts speaking crisply: "It's hard to explain to you, but we have different priorities in this country. After the famine in the mid-nineties, which was the result of a combination of floods and drought along with the American imperialists' trade embargo, we realized that we had to protect our country at all costs and fend for ourselves. From 1988 on, our new politics have been called *Songun Chongchi*. This means the military comes before all else: before the other citizens, before healthcare and everything else. Previously, the workers were the most important group; but if the workers can't defend themselves against the imperialists, everything will fall apart. So now we say, 'Military First.'"

Mr. Song doesn't say anything else about the hierarchy of the rest of the population. But the distribution of aid by international organizations during the second half of the 1990s illustrated how each level of North Korean society is valued according to their degree of usefulness. When Oxfam, Doctors Without Borders, and Doctors of the World realized how cynical the system of distribution was, they left the country.

In North Korea, the population is divided into classes, like a modern caste system organized around people's genealogy. A person's place in the class system is finite; it not only determines food rations but where you live, your career, your privileges, and your general standard of living.

The highest echelon — the "core" class — is made up of members of the Workers' Party of Korea. In the next group are workers, farmers, engineers, teachers, and regular soldiers. This category is called the "wavering" class. The lowest level, the "hostile" class, is made up of fifty-one under-classes, which include, among others: relatives of people who collaborated with the Japanese before 1945, political prisoners, and dissidents. Intellectuals who were forced to come to North Korea during the Korean War, shamans, clairvoyants, and descendants of *gisaeng* (the Korean equivalent of geishas) are also included. One of the lower castes is called *kotchebi* ("swallows") and is made up of orphaned children and youth. The swallows flit through cities in search of food and form criminal gangs to support themselves by pickpocketing.

Class is determined by the bloodline rule that Kim Il-sung established in 1972. This edict can be traced back to a Confucian tradition: a person is responsible for the last three generations of his ancestors. "Factionalists or enemies of class, whoever they are," said the leader, "their seed must be eliminated through three generations."

Between 1995 and 1998, starvation aided this eradication. Mr. Song talks about floods, drought, and trade embargoes as reasons for the catastrophe, but in a functioning society 5 to 10 percent of the population does not die because of difficult weather conditions. In Barbara Demick's book *Nothing to Envy*, a defector who was a teacher in Chongjin recounts how several of her five- and six-year-old students died of starvation during these years, yet she was still expected to get the children to praise the leader every day. Mr. Song doesn't mention any of this, but an older guide in another group told a tourist the other day that his son died during the famine — and this tragic statement was shocking for its candour.

It's hard to understand how an industrialized society that had achieved some level of prosperity could fall so fast. Insight into what actually happened has only recently come to light through the stories of defectors. In *This is Paradise!: My North Korean Childhood*, Hyok Kang gives an eyewitness account of how the famine mercilessly ravaged her classmates:

> The poorest lived on nothing but grass, and during class their stomachs rumbled. After a few weeks their faces began to swell, making them look well nourished. Then their faces went on growing until they looked as though they had been inflated. Their cheeks were so puffy that their view was impeded, and they couldn't see the blackboard. Some of them were covered with impetigo and flaking skin.
>
> As time passed, there were fewer and fewer of us sitting at the school desks.

When the economy collapsed in 1995, the strict social code that held citizens in the state's iron grip relaxed. People stopped going to work, and workplaces were looted of supplies and equipment that could be traded for food. Defectors have told stories of soldiers roaming the city streets and countryside in search of something to eat, how they robbed civilians and got into shoot-outs with the police, and how corpses were left on the stairs of train stations. In his autobiography Hwang Jang-yop, the creator of Juche Thought, testifies that during the worst period cannibalism was rife and human flesh was sold on the black market as "beef." It's possible that the assertion of widespread cannibalism is exaggerated, even if most North Korea experts agree that it did occur.

AFTER MR. SONG's sudden disclosure about military-first politics, we are taken to Warehouse No. 1, a store exclusively for tourists, which is a relatively new thing in Pyongyang. You can buy ginseng, paintings, porcelain figurines, and a number of beauty products. Ari takes pictures of everything. Andrei is drawn to the liquids like a divining rod. With his slightly turbid eyes, he scrutinizes the containers. He spends a long time holding a bottle of alcohol containing a dead snake. He meets the animal's gaze through the glass.

We buy Kaesong Koryo Insam—brand face cream and aftershave, which is spiked with ginseng root. The brochure explains that the creams are good for the brain's health, for the heart, and for the blood vessels. Moreover, the brochure clarifies, the cream is nothing short of a miracle. It protects against cancer, radiation poisoning, and AIDS.

* * *

BY 1983, CHOI EUN-HEE had been in North Korea for five years. For the last four, she hadn't been invited to the Friday parties in the palace. But one day she received another invitation.

It was the sixth of March. It turned out to be an enormous banquet with over one hundred guests and magnificent floral arrangements. Madame Choi was the guest of honour and Kim Jong-il was unusually animated. He delivered a speech in which he christened her the mother of North Korea, mother of Joseon. He said that Korea was made up of a people with the same history and the same culture.

Then the impossible happened. Her ex-husband, Shin Sang-ok, arrived, surrounded by dignitaries. Madame Choi stood and stared at Shin, and all the party guests stared too.

Finally, Kim Jong-il exclaimed: "Why are you standing there? Go on, give each other a hug!"

The guests applauded.

Kim Jong-il then turned to Shin. "Comrade, we would like you to elevate our film industry. From here on you will be our official adviser."

Fresh applause. Kim Jong-il continued: "Let's arrange a wedding for you two. The fifteenth of April, the Great Leader's birthday."

More applause.

Kim Jong-il had held Madame Choi prisoner and nearly drained the life from Shin. Now he was crowning them king and queen of the North Korean film industry and had put himself in charge of planning their wedding, even though they were divorced.

When they sat down, Kim Jong-il took Shin's hand, placed it on his knee, and squeezed it.

"I'm sorry for having caused you so much agony. But no one has touched a hair on Madame Choi's head. Now I'm returning her to you exactly as she was. Mr. Shin, we Communists are *pure*, isn't that so, comrade?"

The surrounding guests mumbled approvingly. The cognac flowed, and the party lasted until three in the morning.

SHIN WAS DEEPLY weary. After his escape attempt, he had been locked in the isolation cell, where it was impossible to lay down. The prison was a panopticon, which made it possible for the guards to always keep an eye on him. As soon as he tried to shift into a new position, they screamed at him. This was supposed to cleanse him of his sins against Kim Il-sung and Kim Jong-il. He stared at the stone wall and thought about film—about films that had already been made and about future films. He thought about the film about Genghis Khan that he wanted to make. That was what kept him alive.

AFTER BEING REUNITED with Madame Choi, Shin was put on a two-week revitalization program of herbal medicines. Like Choi, he had to go through ideological re-education. Shin was back in shape by October, and he quickly began working in high gear, just like the good old days in South Korea.

Miraculously, Shin Films was resurrected in North

Korea, and on a much grander scale. The couple was given an enormous budget, and a film studio was built outside of Pyongyang for them, in addition to the existing Korean Film Studio. They also had unlimited access to extras.

Soon, the film studio had nearly 1,800 employees. But the first feature produced by Shin in North Korea was filmed in Prague. *An Emissary of No Return* (*Doraoji annu milsa*) was the first North Korean film to be shot outside the country. It tells the story of the diplomat Yi Jun, one of the greatest heroes and martyrs of the resistance to the Japanese occupation. Prague is supposed to represent The Hague, where Yi Jun tried to reverse the 1905 treaty that placed Korea under Japanese rule. For the first time, a North Korean film featured Westerners—both in major roles and as extras. Before then, Westerners had been played by North Koreans, who dyed their hair blond.

The next films on the slate were all made that same year (1984), and were shot in the studio lot: the musical *Love, Love, My Love* (*Sarang sarang nae sarang*) and the historical drama *Runaway* (*Talchugi*). In one scene in *Runaway*, Shin wanted to show the anti-Japanese guerillas blowing up a train with dynamite. But instead of building models and using special effects, the authorities gave him an actual train that he could explode on camera.

By now, Shin and Choi were sleeping only three or four hours a night. In a way, they were happy again.

* * *

ANOTHER MONUMENT IS on the itinerary for the afternoon: the Mansu Hill Grand Monument, where a statue of Kim Il-sung, twenty-two and a half metres tall, gazes out over Pyongyang. Behind it, on the wall of the Korean Revolution Museum, is a mosaic that depicts the snow-clad holy revolutionary mountain. We obediently line up again and bow. Elias starts waving to the people, his right hand moving like a propeller. The German North Korean sympathizers arrive with their crocheted vests and beards. None of them greet us.

Mr. Song takes us aside and says in a low voice: "Look at my haircut: a normal, simple centre parting. You see that a lot in North Korea. Nothing strange here."

He explains that North Koreans have better hair growth than Westerners; that they rarely lose their hair, don't go grey, that it grows quickly, and that they have to cut it often. When we're back on the bus we look around at the nineteen other men in our group. Seven are more or less bald; three have significantly thinning hair. And all nineteen are under the age of forty.

Mr. Song is right.

AFTER THE MONUMENT, we are taken to the flower show to admire Kimjongilia and Kimilsungia, blossoms named after the leaders. The first is a blood-red begonia developed by a Japanese botanist; the other is a violet orchid, a gift from Indonesia's President Sukarno when both Kims were visiting in 1965 — the only known occasion that either of North Korea's leaders used a plane to leave the country. Since the trip to Indonesia, the flower has been diligently cultivated. Kimjongilia is said to represent love, justice, wisdom, and peace—words that don't necessarily spring to mind when thinking about Kim Jong-il.

It turns out the weekly flower show is a huge attraction. Arrangements adorned with light and water features shimmer and bubble. There are colourful installations with models of Pyongyang's famous monuments surrounded by flowers. Paintings of Mount Baekdu in different seasons provide the backdrop. Young women in uniforms and families pose for pictures in front of the arrangements. Most people are in brown Home Guard uniforms. Women have bangs and shoulder-length hair that is combed back and fixed in place with the regulation cap. The jackets nip in at the waist.

Women pose, smiling, carefully made up. Over the years, make-up has been one of the few products that North Korean women are able to buy. Cosmetics for women and tobacco for men. The feminine ideal is to be pale and slim; eyebrows are plucked and filled in, and lips are painted red and lined with a contouring pencil.

In *Illusive Utopia*, Kim Suk-young describes North Korea as "a fashion-conscious nation." She means that the design of the uniforms is part of the body politics—that is, part of the aesthetic formation of the nation. It's prescriptive down to the last detail, and it permeates everything from the mass games, parades, theatre, opera, and film to people's everyday clothing. What makes North Korean uniforms unique, she says, is the accentuation of the feminine. She compares them to Chinese revolutionary uniforms, which strove to nullify the differences between the sexes. North Korea went in the other direction, choosing to enhance Woman as a dualistic character. Traditional, virtuous clothing has been preserved and complemented with uniforms that style women as both feminine and military. And the North Korean body politic is an extension of the ruling dynasty's own aesthetic preferences. The leaders visit textile factories, examining fabrics and feeling their quality; they study street life in Pyongyang and give detailed orders about the manufacturing of high heels. At parades, women carry automatic weapons and wear slinky knee-length skirts and tall boots while marching in synchrony, legs lifted high.

The female traffic officers in Pyongyang express the same aesthetic ideal. Their employment contract is like that of a modelling agency. In addition to being beautiful, they have to be at least five feet, three inches tall and unmarried. They are drilled in behaviour and choreography, and the state supplies them with make-up. They have four uniforms, one for each season. During the cold winter of 2005, Kim Jong-il personally saw to it that they were given extra-thick cotton underwear, according to a traffic cop who was interviewed in a Chinese newspaper. Whether Kim Jong-il actually got involved — he is known for being a micromanager — or it's just the North Korean way of speaking, where everything is thanks to the leader, is hard to say.

North Korea even has its own unique fabric. Made from limestone and anthracite, Vinalon, or "Juche fibre" as the product is also called, was invented by the North Korean chemist Ri Sung-gi in the 1930s, while he was still living in Japan. (He returned to Korea of his own volition during the

Korean War.) Full-scale manufacturing began in 1961 under the slogan: "Vinalon is the solution to the clothing problem." Kim Il-sung was excited about this operation, not least because one of its by-products could be used in the manufacturing of chemical weapons, including tear gas, mustard gas, and a poisonous gas that is absorbed by the blood. For a time, most things in North Korea were made of Vinalon. As North Korea expert Bertil Lintner says in *Great Leader, Dear Leader*: They "wake up under their Vinalon quilts and have to put on their Vinalon suits, caps, and canvas shoes before going to work."

MADAME AND SHIN experienced at first hand how clothing was governed from the top down in the fashion-conscious nation. In their joint memoir, they recount the order to wear a hat in the beginning of the 1980s: "The instructions from the Party were religiously followed, so everyone started putting something on their head. Some women wore Western-style hats with a large shade and other women wore hats with ear covers resembling children's hats, all while wearing modified *joseonot*s." On another occasion, when Kim Il-sung had just come home from a trip to Eastern Europe, a message was relayed that men should wear ties. "The next day, everyone was wearing a tie regardless of whether it matched their other clothes or not. People who did not have a dress shirt still wore a tie on top of collarless shirts. From then on, party members and office workers put aside their Mao suits and started to wear ties at work. But Kim Jong-il insisted on wearing a Mao suit."

Kim Jong-il was also deeply involved with Madame's private wardrobe. Rather early on during her imprisonment, he sent her fifty or so boxes of fabric and clothing. There was cashmere for coats, silk for Korean dresses, thin veils, velvet for evening dresses, and three mink coats. Almost every day he sent her boots, hats, and gloves. One of the boxes was filled with make-up. Madame got chills when she saw that all the cosmetics were from her favourite brand. She must have been watched and studied over for a long period of time before the kidnapping.

Kim Jong-il made sure photographers documented her wearing everything he sent. Later, it surfaced that he also knew Shin Sang-ok's shirt size and what his favourite colours were.

* * *

AFTER THE FLOWER show, the bus takes us to the Juche Tower. The 170-metre-tall monument was erected in honour of Kim Il-sung's seventieth birthday, and each stone represents one day of his life. The guide at the site takes us up in the elevator to the observation deck. The sky is clear, and the late-afternoon light is gentle. On one side is the Taedong River. On the other, the view is incomparable: a city devoid of advertising, with very few cars and the odd bicycle like an ant on the street. Pyongyang seems like an aged, sunbleached architectural model made of painted balsa wood and spread out as far as the eye can see. Everything looks orderly from this distance.

The guide, who is dressed in a white *hanbok*, is different from the others we've met: she's a bit older and a bit more charming. She doesn't deliver her talk mechanically; she doesn't tell us where to turn our gazes. She says that her legs are tired from standing all day. Then she chats casually with us. After a while, she falls silent and goes back to pondering the view, a view she sees every day but that she now explores as if there still were nuances left to discover. We ask her about Vinalon and its daily use in North Korea today. Are the Mao suits we see people wearing on the street made from Vinalon? She replies that it's unusual for clothes to be made of the material these days; it's mostly just used for blankets.

She sees the cosmetics in our bags and subtly arches an eyebrow. We've bought the best North Korean beauty products, she assures us. She seems to know what she's talking about.

*   *   *

WE HAVE EATEN dinner and are sitting on the rattan furniture on the outdoor terrace at the Yanggakdo Hotel. Our guides are exhausted. Mr. Song has imposed a collective punishment. The tumult over the course of the day has resulted in us being grounded for the night. The evening walk through the city that was promised has been cancelled.

But right now no one is sorry. Trond has ordered a round of beer for the table. He stands up like a conductor, encouraging everyone to drink. We ask Ms. Kim what she thinks about Trond.

"He's fat," she says.

During the day, the guides struggled to keep the group together. Oksana snuck off several times, happy and carefree. Elias was swept along, consumed with his dream of making contact with the North Korean people. Faced with children and the elderly, his propeller hand was set in motion. They treated him as if he were invisible.

Elias asks detailed questions. He wants to seem like a normal tourist, but his inquiries betray him. In spite of his youth, we think he has probably already reached the limit of what someone can learn about North Korea as an outsider. Now he wants first-hand information. It's not that Elias sympathizes with the regime, quite the opposite in fact. He seems to want to get to the bottom of this crazy country, to witness the monstrous nature of the totalitarian regime. But he is stuck in the gap between what he sees and what he knows.

Half-seriously, half-jokingly Mr. Song asked early on if Elias was with the CIA. Now he's tired of the detailed and endless questions. With a flaring sardonic glint, Mr. Song finally responds: "Too much information can be fatal."

Whether this death threat was what made Elias choose not to partake in the evening's festivities, we don't know, but we do assume that he's trying to uncover all of the hotel's secrets. Among the mysteries is the non-existent fifth floor. It has simply been left out of the Yanggakdo Hotel: in the elevator, there's a jump between buttons four and six. In South Korea, it's the fourth floor that is usually omitted, because the number four symbolizes death.

The Bromma boys claim there's a brothel on the seventh floor. Elias went there and found Mr. Song sitting at a desk just outside the elevator. Elias was immediately shown out. Later, he took the stairs and saw rows of men's and women's shoes lined up outside of the rooms. The eighth floor is also interesting. The employees from the spa, the casino, and the Egyptian-themed disco in the basement spend their free time there. They are all Chinese people from Macao. Hiring North Koreans would be too risky, because of the contact they'd have with foreigners. Ari has managed to get a glimpse of the lives of these Chinese guest workers—men wearing only underwear, stooped over portable gas stoves on the floor—but was promptly shown back to the elevator.

The Bromma boys have their own souvenir from one of the forbidden floors. They've taken pictures of corridors covered in propaganda images. They show us a picture of one of them wearing Ray-Bans and making a peace sign. He's popped the collar of his polo shirt unusually high, like a sea bass flaring its gills. In the background there are pictures of soldiers standing tall, holding machine guns next to the party symbol.

TROND WAVES IN a fresh round of beers. Ari, the flat-cap-wearing Dutchman, stands up, as if Trond will need help conducting the drinkers. We sit at the far, somewhat calmer, end of the table and try to get Ms. Kim to tell us about her life in Pyongyang. Nils, the Gothenburger who lives in Minsk, helps to interpret. It's painfully slow going, even though Nils speaks perfect Russian.

Ms. Kim is wearing a white dress that has a discreet black stripe on the Peter Pan collar. She looks thin and fragile. Her slim wrists seem like they're made from Meissen porcelain. Her father is among the elite. He's been stationed in Novosibirsk, Russia, in order to establish business contacts, on government orders. She says that she likes her language studies and going on walks with her sister, her best friend, and her dog. She and her sister are musical. They both sing and play the piano. In the evenings, they socialize with people their own age at the Kim Il-sung Socialist Youth League. Ms. Kim doesn't like pizza. A movie ticket costs the equivalent of seven pennies. Regarding marriage, everything is very strict. She says that when the time comes, women are twenty-five and the men are thirty. When we question the exact ages, she insists that's how it is.

Farther down the table, one of the Bromma boys vents about how his parents got hit by property tax on their mansion in Stockholm. The six bathrooms were the problem. Thank god the Alliance, Sweden's right-wing government, put a stop to this exploitation of mansion-owners. In his short-sleeved, chicken-yellow Ralph Lauren shirt, red lambswool sweater knotted over his shoulder, shorts, and deck shoes without socks, he seems to have been teleported here from a sailboat that has just docked at some exclusive yacht club.

Two bottles of vodka have materialized and Mr. Song finally starts to relax. Someone brings up the topic of gay clubs. Homosexuality doesn't exist in North Korea, Mr. Song says, and grins at our ridiculousness. The term "gay club" doesn't exist in North Korea. Can, then, the idea of a gay club exist or be understood? Only if it exists in a parallel universe.

One of the Bromma boys gets up, twists the metal cap off the vodka bottle, and calls out to Mr. Song: "Have you heard about Stureplan?"

But Stureplan, Stockholm's famous nightclub area, is definitely out of the bounds of Mr. Song's knowledge.

A light rain, like the mist from a spray bottle, has started to fall. A dark, shifting shadow crosses the light above the bar. An owl has landed on a ledge on the hotel's façade and is quietly observing the goings-on. Then it disappears into the darkness of Pyongyang.

WE HAVE DECIDED to carry on and go to the karaoke bar in the basement, but make a stop at the men's room first. As we are standing in front of the urinals, the door is kicked open.

"Police!" Mr. Song shouts.

The vodka has gone to his head. His face is puffy; he laughs heartily at his own joke. He's glad to have shepherded his flock back to the hotel, where we can't sneak off. Maybe Mr. Song is a policeman. They say one of the two guides is always a policeman. But, who knows, maybe Ms. Kim is the cop?

In the lobby we bump into Antonio Inoki, a Japanese professional wrestler and mega-celebrity whom we recognize from Japanese beer commercials. He kindly obliges to having his picture taken by the hotel guests. He sports a camel-hair coat, a red silk scarf, and a strong jawline. His enormous chin is his calling card and has earned him the nickname "the Pelican."

We don't approach Inoki or ask him to punch us in the face, which in Japan is considered to be the highest honour, almost like a blessing. The whole thing started when Inoki was visiting a school and a student punched him twice in front of the cameras. Inoki smacked the student so hard it knocked him to the ground. The student dizzily clambered up to his feet, bowed, and thanked him. He was a huge, long-time Inoki fan. The incident was replayed on television again and again, and since then celebrities and members of the public alike have requested the blessing of the "Antonio Inoki bitch-slap," as it's called in Japan.

Inoki's master was the Korean Kim Sin-rak. During the occupation, Kim Sin-rak was adopted and raised by a Japanese family. At the end of the 1930s, he transformed into Rikidōzan, the first and greatest of all wrestling stars. His way of smacking down "American crooks" in show matches made him incredibly popular in Japan and also in Korea. Rikidōzan, who died young in 1963 after a fight with a yakuza at a nightclub in Tokyo, is still celebrated as one of the greatest anti-imperialist heroes in North Korea. Moreover, he still has blood ties in the country: his son-in-law is in the North Korean Ministry of Defence. In 1995, a comic book was published that explained that the wrestling star was a hero and eternally famous because Kim Il-sung and Kim Jong-il had embraced him. But the blessing was mutual. During his life, Rikidōzan gifted a limousine to Kim Il-sung.

The man with the giant chin in the lobby was once Rikidōzan's apprentice. Apprentice Inoki has long since reached mastery. He's successfully merged the theatrical pretend-fights in wrestling rings with exhibition matches against judo stars and boxers. In Iraq, Inoki was given two golden swords by Saddam Hussein after aiding the negotiation of an exchange of Japanese and Iraqi hostages shortly before the Gulf War. In 1976, he fought Muhammad Ali. To prepare, Inoki had a karate expert temper his chin with repeated blows, and it was the sight of that chin that made Ali tease him with the nickname "the Pelican." The fight degenerated. Inoki fended off Ali's blows by lying on his back and kicking his opponent's shin. When the long match was deemed a draw, the crowd raged.

After paying a visit to Rikidōzan's grave in Japan in 1995, Inoki came to Pyongyang for a highly anticipated wrestling match. The 1st of May Stadium was filled to the brim with an ecstatic crowd who were there to watch Inoki fight the American Ric "the Nature Boy" Flair. A tender assault played out between the two parties; at one point Inoki carried the ageing, platinum-blond Flair in his arms like an infant.

Since then, busts of Antonio Inoki have been sold at the Mansudae Art Studio, the state-propaganda art factory in Pyongyang. Maybe the choreographed violence of wrestling fits within the framework of North Korean propaganda—both are built on the idea of the power of performance, the selective gaze that refuses to be distracted by unwelcome realities.

WE WALK THROUGH the lobby, illuminated by crystal chandeliers, to a darker area where we find a discreet flight of stairs that leads to the underworld. The stairs take us to the Yanggakdo Hotel's basement, which is panelled in grey marble. The ceiling is less than six feet high, and we have to crouch as we move along the corridor.

This is the hotel's hinterland, the cellar of the temple. In the dark passageways we come across strange locales lit up by strip lighting; between them is only twilight. The tenants at each spot seem to be contracted for eternity. As we pass, they look up with expressionless faces. A souvenir store, a snack bar, a sauna, a two-lane bowling hall, a hairdresser's, suddenly an unlit pool, a grocery store, and finally a bookstore selling tomes by the leaders. Time in these catacombs is killed by daydreaming and staring vacantly into space.

We have arrived at our destination, but we've lost Trond, who dematerialized somewhere along the way. Next to the bookstore, red swinging doors lead into a large, dark karaoke bar.

Songs are chosen from padded binders. One of them contains revolutionary songs. Mr. Song and Ms. Kim stick to this binder. Ari and the Bromma boys make selections from the other.

Fresh vodka bottles appear on the table. The Bromma boys stand up and start bellowing out Aqua's "Barbie Girl." After that, Mr. Song and Ms. Kim take the mike and sing a duet about the triumph of global socialism. Mr. Song, red in the face and flailing his arms, encourages us to sing along. Then it's time for more bellowing. Having downed large glasses of vodka, Ari is bleating like a sheep to Duran Duran's "A View to Kill." He throws his head back, the microphone at his mouth, but the flat cap doesn't budge. We've never seen him without it.

Ms. Kim looks happy when she gets to sing her Korean love ballads and songs of praise to the leader. When she's done, she sits quietly on the edge of the sofa and waits her turn. The Bromma boys jump up and down on the dance floor. They tear off their polo shirts and lambswool sweaters and swing them above their heads, bare-chested.

DAY 6

THE PERFECT FILM

I N A 2006 article, the Swedish journalist and author Richard Swartz asked why dictators are so hard to prosecute. Dictators never seem to leave any tracks: no signatures on documents, no records of commands, no protocol. A dictator's political duty seems to be doing nothing. Mostly, he eats, sleeps, "dances with young girls" (Mao), and sinks into his dreams. Kim Jong-il rarely appears in public and has actually never addressed a large crowd in person.

Sequestered within the high walls of their palaces and hidden from peering eyes are personal infotainment centres and orgiastic amusement parks. Here, dictators live out their comfortable lives and let their underlings handle the executive duties. In these protected worlds, attendants try to interpret every clearing of the throat and every sigh. Given the capricious nature of the dictator, it's no easy job. When anything goes wrong, subordinates are blamed immediately for their misreading, and in this way the leader satisfies his need for traitors.

Swartz thinks that the idle behaviour of dictators is a conscious choice: "The dictator avoids the finality of paper and ink which would make him responsible for his actions." But another reason for this untethered existence could be that the dictator realizes that the true display of power happens on an incorporeal level—that one first and foremost rules through a collection of ideas held by the people themselves, ideas that are maintained with iconography. And so it is best to keep as low a profile as possible. As the playwright Jean Racine wrote: "One might say that the respect we have for heroes increases in proportion to their distance from us." The dictator lets the symbols do their job, symbols that follow people like shadows, that descend on their consciousnesses and keep vigil over their thoughts.

The widely disseminated official portraits, the gigantic banners, Mao's face on Tiananmen Square—these symbolic representations transform the leader into an icon at an incorporeal level. The same goes for monuments. In *What Am I Doing Here?* British author Bruce Chatwin says that all nations fixate on a ceremonial centre, which almost invariably carries celestial overtones. These places invoke the divine in order to sanction a ruler's authority on earth: the Temple of Heaven in Beijing, Red Square, St. Peter's Basilica, the Versailles of the Sun King, and the Great Pyramid, "to say nothing of the installations at Cape Kennedy." The symbolic centre replaces the leader's name.

The leader's face is transformed into a symbol that

belongs to a superhuman sphere. In Mao's case, this is a soft, rolling landscape with a pleasing elevation, a perfectly circular birthmark between his lower lip and his chin, accenting the smooth, powdered hills of his cheeks and his thin, sensitive lips. It is the face of an innocent child and a wise old man. It is both masculine and feminine. The day that the portrait is removed from the entrance of the Forbidden City is the day that China's total transformation into a capitalist superpower will have been openly acknowledged.

THE DESIRES OF a dictator's physical body must be kept secret. Most importantly, his ailments and physical atrophy can never be acknowledged. Ideally, he will travel with a large number of doppelgangers so as to be everywhere and nowhere at once, and always beyond the reach of assassins. In a 2006 article titled "Military-First Teletransporting," the North Korean newspaper *Rodong Sinmun* claimed that Kim Jong-il has the ability to be in several places at once. It stated that Kim Jong-il, "the extraordinary master commander who has been chosen by the heavens," appears in one place only to then suddenly appear at another, "like a flash of lightning."

The locus of power must be untouchable, information has to be censored, and any leaks must be prevented. Of course it's not a given that the dictator engages in orgies of food and drink. He may simply — like Hitler — make endless offers of tea and cake and small talk, as Albert Speer recalled in an interview with Gitta Sereny.

Whatever the degree of debauchery, the dictator's palace is still just home to a withered old man's body. Think of the ageing astronaut in Stanley Kubrick's *2001: A Space Odyssey*, who is revealed after the viewer travels through the many passages and barriers of time and space. On a white rococo bed in a room bathed in greenish light lies a shrunken figure, as dry and lifeless as a mummy.

* * *

WE'VE BEEN WAITING for the bus in the parking lot at the Yanggakdo Hotel for half an hour. We received advance instructions about today's dress code: a collared shirt and long pants. We're going to visit Kim Il-sung's mausoleum and have therefore been asked to dress with dignity. Some of the group are wearing suits and ties. The only one who stands out is Trond, who didn't bring any long pants with him. One of us is wearing a collarless, velvet Hollington jacket, and the other a vintage 1970s blue safari jacket made from synthetic material. It's the closest we have to Maoist suits in the West.

It's nine in the morning on our sixth day and the irritation is rising. The Bromma boys are missing and we're not allowed to leave without them. After another ten minutes, one of them shows up, tired and pale yet freshly washed. With a neutral expression he informs us that his two friends are missing, as if it's the most natural thing in the world. Mr. Song has been on the brink of a meltdown for a long while and rushes off the bus. After another ten minutes, he returns, his face flushed, with the two other Bromma boys skulking behind him.

One says to anyone who will listen: "I'm in the shower and then that fucking Asian just shows up screaming at me." That he and his friends have delayed us for more than an hour doesn't seem to faze him. We hear him in the back of the bus, boasting: "At least I got my shower in."

WE MIGHT MISS the most important stop on this trip: a visit to the Korean Film Studio on the outskirts of Pyongyang. Mr. Song instates "democracy" at this point. We're supposed to vote on whether we'll go to the film studio or the children's palace. We don't have time for both. Luckily, the film studio wins by a few votes. But, before that, we're going to Kim Il-sung's mausoleum.

The mausoleum is housed in Kim Il-sung's enormous palace, the Kumsusan Sun Memorial Palace. This was where he lived and worked—surrounded by architecture fit for a prince. The palace is northeast of the city centre. Two of its sides are protected by a moat.

We enter the imposing building and are sent through a number of stations to prepare for the encounter in the inner chamber. The first is a corridor with rotating brushes that clean the soles of our shoes. Then we arrive at a cloakroom. Someone rips off Ari's flat cap and he blinks as if he has just woken up. It's the first time we have seen his bare head. Next comes the X-ray machine and a metal detector. And then we enter a seemingly endless corridor with a moving walkway.

Kim Il-sung's mausoleum is the primary pilgrimage site for North Korean citizens. We pass hundreds of serious people being whisked along in the opposite direction on the moving walkway. They are all deeply touched by their experience. They're wearing their best clothes and their faces are damp with tears. Our group's presence jars — our posture, the laughing Bromma boys — and many of them seem to regard us with distaste.

We go up an escalator to the next floor. We hear atmospheric music and then a gigantic room opens up before us. At the far end we see an enormous white illuminated statue of Kim Il-sung. The background is lit like a sunrise, the colours transitioning from orange to deep blue. The polished stone floor is like a liquid mirror. It reminds us of the palace in the Emerald City in the *Wizard of Oz*, where Dorothy, the Cowardly Lion, the Tin Man, and the Scarecrow stumble forth and stand trembling in anticipation of their audience with the Wizard.

Mr. Song encourages us to fix our eyes on the statue but not to bow this time, which one would otherwise always do before statues of Kim Il-sung. We are instructed to hold our gazes for sixty seconds and then turn right and go into the next room.

Guides move around the room dressed in *joseonots* made of thick black velvet. They speak incessantly with declamatory voices that every so often crack with despair. On the walls are bronze reliefs that depict groups of grieving people. The marble floor is darker in this room. The specks in the black porphyritic rock glisten, and the female guides say that the floor has been flooded with so many tears that they have turned to crystal.

We are led out of this room into another corridor and

walk through a curtain of air that blasts the dust from our clothes. We then ride an elevator to the antechamber of the most important room: the mausoleum itself. Kim Il-sung's body lays on a catafalque covered by a glass box. Mr. Song gives us careful instructions before we are allowed to approach. We are supposed to walk around the body, bow toward the feet, then to the body's one side and the other, but absolutely not to the head. He doesn't say it outright, but we understand that no living person is considered worthy of bowing to the Great Leader's head.

What we see resembles a wax figure with make-up on: shiny, pale-yellow skin; rouged lips. The North Korean visitors are profoundly affected and many are crying. We can't help but be moved by their solemnity. As a finale, we are allowed to view his belongings: gifts and distinctions that Kim Il-sung was honoured with during his lifetime. Here is the leader's black Mercedes and the train carriage he used when travelling through the country. In one room certificates, medals, and diplomas are on display. There are honorary doctorates in engineering and law from around the world. On the walls are pictures of Kim Il-sung shaking hands with Tito, Arafat, Gaddafi, Assad, Castro, Mubarak...

According to *Daily* NK, it cost 900 million dollars to build the mausoleum. The figure is of course impossible to verify, but undoubtedly they burned through an enormous fortune—and this was during a time when the country was being ravaged by famine. The embalming, which was carried out in a Russian laboratory, is said to have cost one million dollars. Mr. Song says that the North Korean people are willing to offer themselves up for their leader. He says that the palace and everything related to it is a gift from the people.

SOCIOLOGIST MAX WEBER coined the term "charismatic authority." At the time, Weber didn't differentiate between dictators like Hitler and Mussolini and the world's religious leaders, shamans, and certain lunatics. Weber saw unifying characteristics in the magnetism of prophets, heroes, saviours, and political leaders. Charisma isn't so much a trait a leader possesses as it is a product of a relationship between a leader and his followers, Weber said. There's a duty among his subjects to continually hold up the idea of his magnetism. And so the production of charisma starts up, and the leader can take a step back and let the symbols do their job. Even the final exit—death—won't slow this production down.

* * *

THE JAPANESE OCCUPYING powers understood the political importance of film and, in 1920, they established their own studio for pro-Japanese film productions. Japan had occupied Korea since 1905; by 1945 they had made 230 propaganda films, in which Korean identity was covered up or neglected and Japan was imagined as their knight in shining armour. The freedom of Korean filmmakers was limited. In each region of the occupied country, the local police were responsible for monitoring both the films and the audience's reactions. Even film adaptations of traditional folk tales couldn't evade the censors because there was a chance they might be critical allegories of the oppressive regime.

In the 1940s, censorship became even more restrictive. In 1942 all Korean-language films were banned, and from that year until liberation in 1945 only Japanese was spoken in films in Korea. All actors, directors, and anyone else involved were given Japanese names, and any Korean film company could at any point be ordered to make propaganda films for the powers that be.

Back in 1925, a group of writers and artists in southern Korea had established the KAPF (Korea Artista Proletaria Federatio, an Esperanto name). Within the KAPF were socialist guerilla filmmakers who worked under the motto "Art as arms for the class struggle." After completing their fifth feature film, *The Underground Village*, which was about the lives of the poor in Seoul's outskirts, KAPF members were imprisoned and the group was quashed. At the end of the Second World War, when the country was split, some of the surviving KAPF members chose to move to the North to be united with those they felt were their ideological comrades; others decided to stay in the South, and some were abducted by Kim Il-sung's agents. Kim Il-sung had made use of kidnapping as a weapon of war since his days as guerilla soldier in Manchuria.

The KAPF filmmakers soon fell out of favour with the North Korean government. Im Hwa, one of those who had been kidnapped, was executed after being accused of pro-Japanese activities. The others were branded as revisionists and anti-revolutionaries and were written out of the official historical record.

The tendency toward melodrama in North Korea has given their propaganda its own voice: a declamatory, high-pitched voice. This special inflection in speech has long been parodied in South Korea. This distinctive voice isn't just used for propaganda; it has been adopted in everyday speech. Or, if you will, it has infected communication at every level. Films, songs, speeches, official messages—all forms of address are delivered in this tone.

*   *   *

IN THE 1980s, most people in South Korea believed that Choi Eun-hee and Shin Sang-ok had gone to North Korea of their own volition. In 1984 Choi Eun-hee won the Special Jury Prize as Best Director at the Karlovy Vary International Film Festival for *An Emissary of No Return,* even though it was Shin who was the director. He had given credit to her because he wasn't fully pleased with the film. That same year, the couple appeared on Yugoslavian and Czechoslovakian television and said that they had moved to North Korea out of their own free will. Of course they were actually being forced to participate in the charade.

Oddly enough, they also did some shooting in the West. They rented the legendary Bavaria Film Studios in Munich for the fantasy film *The Tale of Shim Cheong,* a musical based on an ancient Korean myth about a princess living in a kingdom at the bottom of the sea. Shin actually already made one version of this myth in South Korea in 1972. Seven North Korean guards watched every step they took during production.

Madame Choi and Shin had become an unmistakable part of the elite, and Kim Jong-il seemed to think that they had found their place.

ON ONE OCCASION, Madame and Shin decided to smuggle a tape recorder into a meeting with Kim Jong-il. They wanted proof that they hadn't come to North Korea of their own volition, proof that they could bring with them on the day they succeeded in escaping.

At the meeting, Kim Jong-il speaks openly about how he was "forced" to bring them to North Korea. An important part of the country's social structure was failing, and he had to take care of it, he explained. He needed to re-establish artistry in film. "I acknowledge that we lag behind in film-making techniques," he said. He added that bringing them to North Korea wasn't actually weighing on his conscience. But he excused himself anyway, saying: "We're all part of the same nation, the land of the Joseon era."

* * *

THE STUDIO IS deserted and the giant buildings rest on their secrets. An office complex surrounds an area that resembles a town square large enough to hold an army of film workers. The studio guide says that the filmmakers are currently on location.

A bronze sculpture group stands on the square. It depicts Kim Il-sung in an overcoat, his arms resting tenderly on a little girl's shoulders. Her hair is braided and she is smiling. Her small hand grips one of the leader's index fingers. A film crew are to the right, cameras ready, and seem to be awaiting instruction, notepads and pens at hand. To the left are the girl's parents, who look proudly on as their daughter is embraced by the Great Leader. They wait subserviently for the moment they can present him with a basket of flowers. There is no doubt that the filmmaking will sprout from the Great Leader's advice. But right now, the leader is busy. A little girl with braids has crossed his path. She is a representative of the child race, so the leader drops everything to speak to her, and the filmmakers wait patiently for his instructions.

The bus takes us to the backlot to view the sets. They aren't really sets, but actual houses that have been built in a variety of styles. The guide points out that, this way, you can shoot from more angles. At the first stop we are allowed to view a few buildings that are meant to look like they are from the late Joseon period. To our dismay, we are immediately offered the opportunity to try on clothing from the costume department. Andrei is transformed into a feudal lord with a yellow silk cape, a hat, and a fake beard. Suddenly he perks up. He slowly stalks about the muddy ground with a regal expression, waving his arms theatrically, before taking his place on a wobbly wooden throne. The Bromma boys have found some wigs; the chubby one pulls on a bright red wig that makes him look like a bloated, grown-up Pippi Long-stocking. They flank Andrei and make faces for the camera.

AFTER THIS EXCRUCIATING scene, we are finally allowed to see the various towns that have been constructed for film shoots. We see the muddy streets of the studio's vision of Seoul at the time of the Japanese occupation. Another set depicts a decadent nightlife area in Tokyo; naive scenery portrays immoral life in modern-day Seoul. There is a bucolic Asian farming idyll from an unspecified time, and a Bavarian village — the illusion is successful at a distance but then you get closer and see that the houses are made of reinforced concrete. The average North Korean citizen's ideas about the world have been shaped by these sets.

We take pictures of the signs in the studio town: the "Oasis" bar; "Happy Toothpaste," a store that sells nylon underwear; "Fujicolor," painted by a shaky hand. Korean and Chinese characters are used for these establishments. On a sign for a leather-goods store, all of the shoes and handbags are depicted as if they have fallen into a corner. Life in the West is brazenly luxurious. LUXURIOUS SHIRTS, TIES, SUITS AND MAKE-UP, proclaims one sign. Another advertises something as superfluous as pet accessories. A funny dog wearing sunglasses, a pearl necklace, and a hat is painted on it. Another sign is even more peculiar: WOMEN'S WRESTLING CLOTHES.

The film posters on advertising columns are hand-painted. They illustrate versions of real films. Elements of famous movies have been mashed up, the casting has been changed, and they've created imaginary hybrid films. *The Seven Year Itch* shows a portrait of a woman who looks more like Jeanne Moreau than Marilyn Monroe. *Giant* features new actors: Clark Gable and Jane Russell instead of James Dean and Elizabeth Taylor. *Treasure Island* has the British actor Robert Newton in the lead as in the real film, but he's acting opposite an unknown co-star: "Linda Danelle."

*   *   *

WE IMAGINE THAT if we had been in this film studio exactly twenty-four years ago, in September 1984, we would have encountered an unusual rubber costume hanging on a stand. It resembles an armadillo standing on its hind legs. In a farming village, a forge is being built. It's supposed to be a feudal village in the 1300s, during the Goryeo dynasty, even if the architecture isn't strictly of its time.

A Japanese film crew from Toho Studios in Tokyo has just arrived. The group comprises a number of special effects artists, along with suit actors Kenpachiro Satsuma and the diminutive Masao Fukazawa — stage name "Little Man Machan" — a former wrestling star and the embodiment of Godzilla's son, Minilla. They have brought a large load of Styrofoam because this material isn't available in North Korea. It will be used to make boulders that will be rolled down into a ravine in order to crush the Imperial Army.

The monster's head, with its evil grin, lies on the ground next to the stand with the rubber suit. Little Man Machan, who is barely four feet tall, climbs a ladder so he can take the suit down from its stand. His head sticks up out of the rubber torso and Satsuma crowns it with the monster's head.

Little Man Machan takes a few unsteady steps in the stiff, cumbersome costume, and struggles to raise his arms. The monster springs to life.

KIM JONG-IL HAD the fantastic idea of copying a concept from his arch-enemy, Japan. He thought a *kaiju* (monster) movie might unite the nation, and in the frenzy around the film, the monster itself would become an idol. The creature could be spread to the masses in the form of a plastic toy. And best of all, a message could be embedded in this adventure — a message that would fill the people with courage. The movie would bear the monster's name: Pulgasari.

How the Toho crew had ended up in North Korea was something of a mystery. Satsuma himself wrote about the events in his autobiography *I Am the Actor*. He strikes a trickster-like pose on the cover, resembling a Toshiro Mifune lookalike, and his tone is self-regarding. In his filmography, pornography and comedies are listed alongside his many monster films. But he doesn't mention Little Man Machan's alleged behind-the-scenes involvement in the production of *Pulgasari*. Rumours of connections to the Japanese mafia swirled around the diminutive actor.

According to Satsuma, the Toho crew thought they were en route to Hollywood for an assignment, but just before they departed they were told they were supposed to shoot in North Korea instead. Along with their boss Mr. Suzuki, one Mr. Kazuo Kinagawa from Hong Kong had taken care of the arrangements. The Hong Kong man clearly was an employee of Kim Jong-il. Whether he tricked Mr. Suzuki or bribed him, Satsuma doesn't say.

After one week of filming in a studio in Beijing, the Toho crew arrived in Pyongyang. The crew members were chauffeured in Mercedes Benzes on empty roads that had no traffic lights and they spent the night in one of Kim Jong-il's private residences. Satsuma describes his surprise upon seeing the studio. The newly built four-storey building had 300 rooms.

THE TOHO CREW was quartered in a first-class hotel in central Pyongyang. The rooms had brick-red walls and moss-green, wall-to-wall carpeting, as well as trouser presses and marble bathtubs. Breakfast was always the same: toast that crumbled as soon as you touched it, goat milk, fried radishes, bacon, eggs, and apples. In the evenings, they'd grab a drink in the hotel bar. The prices were unpredictable. One whisky could cost 2,000 yen (about 8 dollars), the same price they'd pay for the whole crew's tab on another night. Other times it was free.

Phone calls home were allowed only if they were requested a week in advance, but they were permitted to watch NHK, Japan's national television station. After a month they were downgraded. The Mercedes were replaced with Volvos, and the crew was moved to a more modest hotel.

But the strangest part of the whole situation was that the director was the famous South Korean Shin Sang-ok. And his celebrity actress-wife Madame Choi sometimes appeared on set. Why was South Korea's leading director of melodrama filming a *kaiju* movie in Pyongyang? He'd left for the North, they knew, but had he been bribed or forced? They could do nothing but speculate. No one dared to ask.

*   *   *

BEFORE WE ENTER the studio's sound stage, the guide says that Kim Jong-il often comes here and gives solid advice. To us, the advice sounds a bit general: "Preserve these buildings and use them more effectively." The guide says that North Korean filmmakers sometimes experience doubt and insecurity. In moments like these it's good to have a stable, firm authority to lean on. They phone Kim Jong-il and get answers to their questions. This is how one makes a "perfect film."

The sound stage has seen better days. If you don't take the worn wooden scenery flats and the abraded bucket seats into account, the studio takes you right back to the 1980s. As far as we can tell, the latest sound technology at that time was installed in the screening room. But they haven't upgraded since it was built.

A film that is in the process of being mastered starts to play on the screen. It begins with the logo of the North Korean film industry, which we recognize from *Pulgasari's* opening credits and the large mosaic on the studio square. The symbol depicts a sculpture in Pyongyang: the winged horse Chollima, a Korean pegasus leaping into the future. According to the folk tales, the Chollima can run 400 kilometres in a day and no knight could ever tame it. In the terminology of the revolution, "Chollima-speed" is the speed with which North Korean society surges forth. The Chollima Movement in the 1950s was the North Korean answer to Mao's Great Leap Forward.

A montage of documentary and feature-film scenes about the war against Japan follows the Chollima logo. There are arrogant Japanese businessmen with round glasses and Hitler moustaches, slaves working in a quarry, and gangsters wearing pinstriped jazz suits. We recognize the actors' gestures from North Korean dramas: someone falls on the ground and reaches up his arm in anguish; someone wipes the sweaty, bloody foreheads of the dying; families and lovers are torn apart, crying and screaming.

We are gripped by the feeling that we are nearing the heart of the story. This could be the command centre of our story. We are rapt, but our fellow travellers are silent and bored. Even Elias seems distracted. In the darkness, we hear someone snoring.

WITH AWE AND wonder, Shin and Madame watched the studio grow. They couldn't help but feel flattered; Kim Jong-il offered them resources that they'd never have dreamed of before. But every day they discussed their escape. They mapped out their flight like the plot twists in a screenplay, but they also knew that their plan could never be realized.

*   *   *

WE LEAVE THE film studio with the feeling that something that has slipped through our fingers. Maybe we'd convinced ourselves that we could find solid evidence of Madame and Shin's time there? Perhaps a dusty monster head in a prop closet? Pulgasari's grimacing, horned mask?

Our bus travels south, passing Pyongyang's enormous triumphal arch, which is of course several metres taller than the original Arc de Triomphe in Paris, and we soon find ourselves on the Reunification Highway that leads straight as an arrow to Kaesong, right on the border with South Korea. There are four lanes with a green belt in the middle. After a while, we realize that we've never been on a highway like this before; hardly any cars are on the road. We pass a few military vehicles, and amid much irritated honking we overtake a crowded bus, but otherwise it's empty.

We see a few people doing maintenance along the road — micro-maintenance. One woman is sweeping up a pile of dry leaves and dust on the road. She squats and lifts the debris with her cupped hands, then tosses it over the barrier guard into the ditch.

ON THE BUS ride, we look at the pictures of the production of *Pulgasari* in Kenpachiro Satsuma's memoir. There are interior shots of the hotel in Pyongyang where they stayed, as well as of restaurants, grocery stores, and department stores. The department store was a copy of one in Japan and offered both Japanese and black market goods. The staff even smiled and offered perfect greetings of *"sumimasen"* ("excuse me"), exactly as they did in Tokyo. In the hotel there was a camera store where the shopkeepers spoke accent-free Japanese. It was assumed that a number of the employees were Japanese citizens who had been kidnapped.

Until recently, North Korea has officially denied the kidnapping of Japanese people. For twenty years, their protesting relatives were considered dogmatists, even in Japan. No one believed them. But in 2002 Kim Jong-il admitted to the abduction of thirteen Japanese citizens, five of whom were allowed to go home. The Japanese government's official list contains the names of seventeen citizens (including the five who have returned), but organized groups of relatives claim that as many as eighty people are being held captive in North Korea. The question has become especially sensitive since Japan's right-wing nationalists appropriated the matter in order to make a case for remilitarization.

It is known that people from a number of countries, including Romania and Thailand, have been abducted and taken to North Korea. During her time in the country, Madame met people who had been kidnapped from Jordan, Japan, and France. South Korea insists that 480 of its citizens are being held in North Korea against their will.

In 2002, Hitomi Soga was allowed to return to Japan. She was nineteen years old when she and her mother were kidnapped in 1978. They were taken on board a boat and ferried to Nampo and then on to Pyongyang. She married Charles Robert Jenkins, an American commander who willingly crossed the border at the demilitarized zone (DMZ).

During the first half of the 1960s, a total of four American soldiers sought happiness in the North, where they all became players in a large-scale theatre of propaganda. At least one of them had the threat of martial law hanging over his head at the time of his defection. Joe Dresnok, the only one who still lives in North Korea, appeared in the British documentary *Crossing the Line* in 2007.

North Korea heralded the arrival of the four military defectors: Dresnok, Charles Jenkins, Larry Abshier, and Jerry Parrish. Brochures about these "Fortune's Favourites" were printed along with photographs of the men picnicking by the river with local beauties, bottles of wine, and teeming picnic baskets. Their clothing was suspiciously similar. North Korean tailors must have projected their own idea of what American men would wear on a Sunday outing: uniform-like turquoise suits, straw hats, shirts with wide collars and giant buttons, all presumably made of Vinalon.

The soldiers were presented like trophies: they appeared at mass meetings, and relayed messages via the loudspeakers that were broadcast across the border. These siren songs from paradise were aimed at the understimulated American troops on the south side who were waiting for action; in the Communist country, everyone was given free food and shelter and unlimited access to women.

But the four Americans were idle, even if they were supplied with steady food rations and alcohol, despite what was happening in the rest of the country. Dresnok describes a largely carefree existence: studying Kim Il-sung's writings, playing cards, drinking *soju*, and taking fishing trips by the river.

According to Charles Jenkins, it wasn't as idyllic as all

that. Until 1972, the men lived in a one-room apartment without running water. They got on each other's nerves, and Dresnok was a brutal fellow who often gave Jenkins a good hiding. When they were separated in 1972, the situation improved. Dresnok and Jenkins started teaching English, but Jenkins, who was from North Carolina, spoke with a deep Southern accent. When it was apparent that future spies had parroted Jenkins's thick regional dialect, he was fired.

ONLY WHEN KIM JONG-IL became the minister of propaganda did the state find a use for these men, who would have been called "hillbillies" back home. Around the time of Madame's kidnapping, the propaganda minister started production on the TV series *Unsung Heroes*. The destinies of the four soldiers were only revealed to the United States in 1996, when the CIA acquired a copy of *Unsung Heroes* and analyzed the voices of the actors.

THE TV SERIES takes place during the Korean War. At its centre is a North Korean agent who stymies the South Korean and American imperialists. Donning aviators and a moustache, Joe Dresnok faithfully embodies the role of the cruel camp commander and lead interrogator Arthur Cockstud. The others were typecast in their roles but had a chance to refine them over the course of the series: Jerry Parrish played a freedom-loving Irishman who hated the Brits; Larry Abshier was the American stooge; and the poisonous spider — Jenkins's character, with his pronounced forehead, wingnuts for ears, and large hat—was the sly American architect of evil behind the war.

Playing the roles of evil American imperialists, they all became film stars in North Korea. Today, people who meet Joe Dresnok on the streets of Pyongyang still call him Arthur. When a copy of *Unsung Heroes* was screened in South Korea, the theme song "Welcome Happiness" became a minor hit. In 2005 when South Korea's minister of culture visited North Korea, he started to sing the theme song during a dinner. A popular move in North Korea. Less so in the South.

WE'RE HALFWAY TO Kaesong and are about to make a pit stop. The bus driver doesn't go to the trouble of pulling into a parking lot; he just pulls up at the side of the road. We automatically look left and right before we cross the highway to get to the rest stop, but it's completely unnecessary.

The café barely has anything to purchase, and the stench of urine in the washroom is stupefying. When we get back on the bus we sit right at the front to film the rest of the journey south. In the beginning we had discreetly used our camera; now we've changed tactics. Mr. Song is surprisingly lax about this. When we pass military posts, he asks us to turn it off; otherwise, he doesn't seem to care much. He says that he's never seen a tourist with such a big camera.

Soon we get back to the topic of hairstyles. Now what did that article say? What punishment did you get for having an incorrect hairstyle?

*   *   *

WE LEAVE OUR baggage at the hotel in Kaesong, which is encircled by a sturdy wall. But the wall doesn't keep out the sound of the many loudspeakers projecting revolutionary music and disciplinary speeches. These speakers are everywhere. Trucks carrying large speakers travel the countryside so that the field workers can get their dose of instruction and warnings. And as if this wasn't enough, in every home a mounted, wired speaker turns on automatically at fixed times. You can turn the volume down, but you can't shut it off. If strangers are on their way to the neighbourhood, local citizens are given instructions on how to behave. Inspectors make rounds to ensure that the home speakers are installed properly and that no one has cut any of the wires. All of the radios in North Korea, except the illegal ones, are manufactured domestically and can receive only the din of transmissions from the state channel.

Kaesong is an unusual city both because we tourists are allowed to visit and because of the economic exchange with South Korea that has been in development for the past few years. Hyundai and a number of other corporations have been allowed to establish factories to produce shoes, watches, clothes, ginseng, and precious stones. Even the electricity in this city comes from the South. But for the moment, our simple hotel doesn't have electricity, nor is there any hot water. And the beds are like those found in traditional Korean hostels: thin mattresses that you roll out on the floor.

This industrial zone was established after North Korea

received a huge donation of money from South Korean businesses, mainly Hyundai. These companies are, of course, interested in the cheap labour the country has to offer. Only citizens approved by the regime are allowed to work in the zone. After a while they are replaced. Their salary is paid to the North Korean state, which in turn pays a share to the workers.

When we found ourselves on the south side of the border a year ago, in June 2007, we saw South Korean trucks transporting sand, waiting to go through the strict border control. They were all issued with small red tattered flags as a mark of courtesy — or perhaps to assimilate them into the North Korean landscape.

IN THEIR BOOK *The Hidden People of North Korea,* Ralph Hassig and Oh Kongdan emphasize the changes that were made to the economy after the country's catastrophic famine. The authors mean that people broke the rules in order to survive; or rather, those who broke the rules were the ones who survived. Previously, North Koreans were paid in coupons — based on their status in society — that could be redeemed for food. But the system stopped working in the mid-1990s and people were forced to scavenge.

Different systems, official and unofficial, exist side by side and overlap in North Korea. To simplify, there are four general frameworks:

1. The official planned economy.

2. A number of enclosed free-trade zones to which international investors have been invited.
3. Small-scale local markets that were previously illegal but have become authorized. These markets—even if they are controlled by the state—have meant a great change.
4. The Kim clan's personal economy, which includes gold mines, heroin and amphetamine production, and the production of counterfeit currency, cigarettes, and pharmaceuticals like Viagra.

The smuggling carried out by North Korean diplomats—which seems to be part of the unofficial job description—is also part of this economy. In 1977, diplomats at the North Korean embassy in Stockholm were deported for engaging in large-scale alcohol and hash smuggling operations. A picture in *Dagens Nyheter* showed a police officer with a confiscated magnum of Dewar's White Label on a serving stand. The diplomats were apparently not smuggling for reasons of personal gain. The proceeds were used to buy full-page ads in the daily newspapers. This was the only way Kim Il-sung's propaganda speeches could find their way into print in the major Western newspapers.

All of these lucrative operations furnish the top echelon with further riches. Bureau 39 in the North Korean Workers' Party organizes the extraction of everything valuable and desirable in the country, like ginseng, precious metals, matsutake, and sea urchins, for the benefit of the elite. Bureau 39 also organizes the manufacturing of narcotics, pharmaceuticals, and counterfeit money. Beyond funding the clan's luxurious lifestyle, it is likely that the bureau's income supports the North Korean nuclear weapons program.

What's remarkable is that the products that come from the country's underground factories outshine the originals. The drugs and pharmaceuticals are considered very potent. And the counterfeit hundred-dollar bills are so well made that the FBI has been forced to admit that they are virtually impossible to distinguish from the originals. In 1996, the U.S. government decided to modify the dollar to counteract the North Korean counterfeit industry. It was the first time since 1928 that the United States Department of the Treasury had been forced to change the banknote. They began using an ink that changed colour in the light, and introduced a new safety thread and a new watermark. It took just two years for the North Koreans to figure out how to copy these new banknotes. Shortly thereafter, new forged hundred-dollar bills were in circulation in casinos in Macao and Las Vegas. Again, changes were made. The Americans invested in a wildly expensive printing press, which they thought would make it unprofitable for the North Koreans to continue counterfeiting, given the investment it would demand. But again they were wrong. New North Korean U.S. dollars were soon out in the market.

In an interview with the *New York Times*, one civil servant at the U.S. Treasury Department dejectedly stated that there is perhaps one way the North Korean hundred-dollar bills can be distinguished from the originals: they are better made.

THE SITUATION IN the industrial zone outside of Kaesong has become more difficult since Lee "The Bulldozer" Myung-bak became president of South Korea in February 2008. To show its displeasure, North Korea tore up signed contracts in protest of the new South Korean government's animosity toward them.

South Koreans are normally denied entry to North Korea except in purpose-built, fenced-off holiday facilities. In Kumgangsan — the Diamond Mountains — in North Korea's Kangwon Province, South Koreans spent a few seasons vacationing at "Hyundai's holiday gulag," with its fresh air and newly built golf course, the largest in Asia. They handed over their cell phones, and cameras were stripped of their powerful zoom lenses. Guests played golf during the day and sang karaoke at night. But exactly two months prior to our visit, a fifty-three-year-old South Korean woman happened to find her way out of the designated area and was shot dead by the North Korean military. Since then, the tourist facilities have been empty.

*   *   *

THE BUS TAKES us through Kaesong's wide streets. We pass a number of military posts and then we are out in the countryside. The sun is low over the landscape. We drive on a narrow road built for tanks. It is made of concrete slabs and cuts through fields where rice, corn, lettuce, and potatoes are being cultivated. Women squat to wash their clothes in a clear stream. It's the weekend, but the worker brigades don't have the day off. Young men holding reaping hooks march in line next to the cornfields, on an elevated path.

Goats gambol in the lush grass, and water buffalo with rings in their noses shut their eyes against the setting sun, dreamily chewing cud. We could be anywhere in East Asia if not for the young girl on a bicycle wearing a red scarf and carrying a backpack with a red flag. She appears to be illuminated by the warm evening light, and she triggers the memory of another image: a Chinese propaganda picture from the Cultural Revolution.

This is most likely one of the most fertile areas in North Korea. Many parts of the country have wretched terrain — mountainous regions where not much can be farmed and which were hardest hit by the famine in the mid-1990s.

A RETIRED COLONEL has joined us on the bus for this excursion. He's wearing a brownish-green decorated uniform and bulky cap bearing a red stripe. The driver stops for some geese on the road. The colonel steps forward, opens the door, and gives their owner a telling off. She looks back at him fearfully, while trying to drive her animals with a cane. The colonel is furious and goes on ranting at the woman, though he seems to be directing his ire just as much at the waddling, unfazed geese.

THE EVENING FOG is starting to rise when we reach our destination: an observation tower in the DMZ. We look around at the rolling, verdant landscape. The tiger has significant symbolic value in Korea, and perhaps the notion that a few

165

Siberian tigers have survived in the DMZ is an expression of the enduring dream that the Korean spirit will reunite North and South. The demilitarized zone is like a wildlife reservation—a sanctuary for a number of rare birds, an unusual breed of wild goat, Amur leopards, lynx, and a few Asian black bears. No tigers have been spotted, but tracks such as claw marks and carrion have been found.

After a short introduction by the colonel, we are invited to look south through a telescope. We are supposed to see a long concrete wall that the South Koreans and Americans built for defence. The wall, the colonel says, was built between 1977 and 1979 and contains hangars with tanks, ready for an invasion. Like the Berlin Wall, this is the symbol of the division of the country, says the colonel. The wall embodies imperialist politics.

But the fog makes it impossible to discern a wall, even with our telescopes. Neither the United States nor South Korea admits to its existence. It seems strange to deny the existence of a five- to eight-metre-tall construction that is said to contain a total of 800,000 tons of cement, 200,000 tons of steel, and 3.5 million cubic metres of gravel and sand. But the North Koreans claim that their enemies have piled up a layer of dirt so that the wall can't be seen from the south side, and have built ramps for vehicles and ground troops. The two countries don't agree on anything that has happened since the Japanese occupation. This extends to fundamentals such as the existence of giant 248-kilometre wall that stretches from west to east.

When we later try to look for pictures of the wall on the

Internet and in other reports, we don't find anything substantial. All tourist groups that visit this observation point seem to arrive just as the evening fog is rising. The photographs that are used to prove the existence of the barrier are reminiscent of pictures of UFOs, where details have been marked with thick lines. When you enlarge these images, you step into a fog of pixels.

THE COLONEL WANTS us to sing on the drive back to Kaesong. After working his way through a melodramatic hit song and then giving the stage to Ms. Kim and her dulcet tones, he walks around the bus with a microphone and tries to coax us all to join in. With the exception of Nils's clear rendition of the classic ballad "Fritiof and Carmencita," no one in the group can sing. Our voices bounce up and down, squalling and screeching.

The Bromma boys, in line with last night's karaoke performance at the Yanggakdo, have cast aside all of their inhibitions; they've crossed some sort of threshold. Everything they experience in North Korea is "totally friggin' awesome." Now they're belting out Swedish left-wing anthems into the microphone: "High Standards" and "State and Capital." One of them transitions to Tenacious D's "Fuck Her Gently," while the others roll around with laughter. The journey back to the hotel is not an easy one.

DAY 7

BACK AND FORTH ACROSS THE BORDER

THE BLUE BARRACK-LIKE buildings in the demilitarized zone are the only place where the military from the North and those from the South can meet face to face. We see a small, plain desk in a room that can't be more than thirty square metres. The border runs right through the middle of this desk.

After some explanation from the guide, we go back to the grand building that constitutes North Korea's watchful eye on the South. From the South Korean side, it's said that the building is actually just a metre-thick façade, but we can confirm that it does indeed contain marble stairs and a sturdy balcony from which we can see tour groups on the southern side. The tourists walk gravely and stiffly along the road to the same blue barracks that we've just visited, but from the other end. They've been told not to make any sudden movements with their arms; this could incite the North Korean military to open fire.

Trond and Ari wave and shout at the tourists. We think they look funny, a solemn line slinking toward the barracks.

THE BIGGEST MILITARY presence in the world is on our side of the DMZ. Last summer, when we toured on the other side of the border, we went down one of the kilometre-long tunnels which the South Korean military had found between 1974 and 1990, and which were probably built for a surprise attack from the North. The so-called "infiltration tunnels," the first of which was discovered when steam was seen rising from the ground, housed railroad tracks and could accommodate the transport of large numbers of troops. Apparently it was there that the Swedish drilling equipment from Atlas Copco, which arrived with the shipment of Volvo cars, was put to use.

In the cold, we stooped so as to not to hit our heads on the stones, which dripped with condensation. The walls were spray-painted black to make it look like a coal-mining tunnel.

Our chief aim in South Korea was a meeting with Choi Eun-hee. After a long period of time, she finally agreed to meet with us in central Seoul.

IT WAS JUNE 2007 and there was a gentle buzz in the JW Marriott Hotel's large lobby. They'd managed to keep out the thick, humid air, and it seemed as if it were being held at bay by the guards at the front entrance, in their white cotton gloves and unusual white storm hats.

Madame Choi had chosen the location. We found a secluded nook in the lobby, a nougat-coloured leather sofa under an oil painting by the Danish artist Ole Ring. We sat quietly, studying the picture, waiting for Madame to appear. It depicted a few country houses in a snowy landscape. In the foreground were a few windswept willows, with every groove in the bark depicted in detail.

Choi Eun-hee arrived, dressed head to toe in black. She wore a hat with an elegant, sloping black brim, large tinted glasses, and a crucifix inlaid with onyx. Her face was considered to have been the first "Western" face in Korean cinema: large eyes, strong eyebrows, and a defined nose.

Madame was seventy-seven years old, but the only things that gave her age away were her hands. She presented us with a gift: a DVD titled *Flower in Hell* (*Jiokhwa*). The 1958 film was the first Korean movie to show a kiss on screen, Madame said. And it wasn't a just a peck, but deep French kissing and groping, and there were wild brawls too. The censors were very strict at that time, but officials must have been sleeping through this one.

Twenty years later, Madame also helped introduce the first kiss in North Korean cinema. In 1984, she and Shin made *Love, Love, My Love*, which is based on "The Legend of Chunhyang," a classic Korean tale about a lower-class woman who marries above her social standing. The kisses in that film were much more chaste, half-obscured by an umbrella, but they still incited strong protestations.

OUR INTERPRETER HAD ordered an iced coffee for Madame, which was placed on the marble table with a discreet clang. Madame rarely gave interviews, and she had abstained from doing any since Shin Sang-ok died in April 2006. But she began speaking methodically, with a deep, soft voice, and she started from the beginning.

At the start of her career, Madame worked in live theatre, getting parts in productions of Molière and Shakespeare. She was given her first film role two years after the Japanese left Korea. One year later, at the age of eighteen, she married a poor cinematographer against her parents' will and "out of pity." Her husband was twelve years her senior and had previously been married to a barmaid who had left him alone with their child. The man turned out to be pathologically jealous.

In the chaos following the outbreak of the Korean War, she was separated from her husband and kidnapped by the Communists. The Communists had taken Seoul, and she was kept in a military camp, where she was forced to perform in propaganda plays for the Red Guards. When the North Korean troops retreated after the arrival of UN forces, they took the actors with them so that the soldiers would be entertained during the march back north. Bombs fell, but the show went on.

However, during an attack by UN troops, Madame managed to escape and make her way back to Seoul. "I was called a collaborator and I was put on trial," she said. "But I was fine. The charges were dropped on one condition: that I entertain the South Korean military."

Madame smiled at the irony.

She looked down at her hand and ran a finger tenderly over her two rings, one silver and the other gold. She began telling us how she fell for Shin Sang-ok. It was 1953, the same year that Shin was working on the film *Korea*, in which the Korean folk tale "The Legend of Chunhyang" was being staged as a "play within a play" in the film. Shin was a young, promising director, and for some time he had admired Madame from afar as a stage actress. He offered her the lead role in the staging of the folk tale.

Meanwhile, Madame's husband had been injured during a bombing in Seoul and was unable to work. She took care of his child and visited him every day at the hospital, but still his jealousy grew. After he beat her with his crutches, she had had enough and left him. It turned out that he had forgotten to register their marriage, which was supposed to have been done in his home village, but the man had been too lazy to make the arrangements when they got married.

Madame and Shin fell in love. They exchanged rings in a love hotel and pledged their eternal devotion. Initially, their marriage caused a scandal. In Korea, a woman's virtue was everything. The press compared Madame to Ingrid Bergman, who left her husband for Roberto Rossellini. Shin tried to convince her not to care about what people thought, but it troubled her.

From the start, they threw themselves into a punishing work schedule. Work, love, and life became one. "We worked twenty-four hours a day," she said. "Film was our life. There were only a few cameras available and we were terrified that they'd be damaged. The cameras were passed from filmmaker to filmmaker. Shin took home the negatives and edited at night. I made costumes and the sets. Many things were reused from film to film."

Choi Eun-hee wasn't like her female colleagues. As soon as she had the chance, she got behind the camera to watch the rushes. As a stage actress, she felt torn about acting without a live audience. She wanted to understand the process and see what the eye of the camera was seeing. At that time, no woman was allowed to touch the camera. Cameras were extremely valuable and women weren't trusted with them. This superstitious attitude was connected to a Confucian tradition, she told us. Back then women weren't allowed to do many things, such as sitting in the front seat of a taxi or in the bow of a fishing boat. It was also inappropriate to get involved in the technical side of filmmaking, but Shin encouraged her. During the second movie they made together, she was already involved in the editing process. But she still wasn't allowed to touch the editing equipment, so she wrote detailed instructions on paper.

Madame had harboured dreams of a quiet life as a housewife, but Shin was totally against it. He didn't want her to spend her time taking care of a household. When she washed clothes, he wondered why she wasn't spending her valuable time reading screenplays.

Shin spoke only of film; everything else was alien to him. During the most intense periods of work he barely ate, and during shoots he didn't even notice when he hurt himself; he was consumed by his vision. He expressed his love for his wife by casting her in his movies. They made many films together, but many more were waiting in his imagination.

"We talked more about film than about life," said Madame.

Shin was oblivious to the world around him unless he could see it as part of a film. The same applied to people. One time, Madame noticed him staring at their sofa. It would fit well into a film that he was working on, he said. The next day, he sent an assistant to pick it up. A little later, she found him staring at her antique bureau. It was a family heirloom, in fact the only heirloom she had. The bureau was close to her heart, and she asked him to leave it be. The next day it was gone. Shin told the crying Madame: "You are also a cinephile, so you can't hate me too much for taking it."

IN THE 1950s, Shin built up a small film production and distribution company called Seoul Films. The financing had its peaks and valleys. Film production was considered a luxury and was heavily taxed. The censors were uncompromising and there were many onscreen taboos. Nothing that touched on the topic of Japan or Japanese rule could pass. She says that the 1955 costume drama *The Youth* (*Jeolmeun geudell*), in which she had the role of a Mata Hari–like character who plots against the Japanese oppressors, was banned and the 1968 film *The Eunuch* (*Naeshi*) — about a king, his concubine, and her lover — was hacked into pieces.

THE FILM COUPLE lived hand to mouth. In 1958 they made *Flower in Hell* on a low budget, purely out of enthusiasm.

Shin was inspired by Italian neorealism, and Vittorio De Sica's *The Bicycle Thief* and Roberto Rossellini's *Rome, Open City* had made a huge impact on him. *Flower in Hell* is about a young man who goes to Seoul to bring his wayward brother back to the countryside, only to become seduced by his sibling's corrupt lifestyle. It was shot on the streets of Seoul and around the U.S. Army barracks, where the prostitutes were. These women wore American 1950s dresses, smoked cigarettes, chewed gum, and drank Budweiser.

Madame plays Sonya, a prostitute who stumbles through the chaotic, sandy environment of the barracks, where jeeps filled with American soldiers stir up dust along the barbed-wire-fenced roads. The barracks are the stomping grounds of pimps and petty thieves, and Sonya is in a relationship with one of the thieves—a gang leader who wants to get their lives in order, move out of Seoul, and live a good, honourable life. For Sonya, this is a hopeless dream. Prostitutes are merely the temporary companions of American soldiers and are considered untouchable by decent Korean society; they occupy a no man's land. As Sonya's friend Judy says: "If we can neither live with the Americans nor the Koreans, then who are we?"

THE COUPLE'S FINANCIAL situation improved at the end of the 1950s, if only temporarily. These were their best years. South Korea's first president, Rhee Syng-man, had built the massive Anyang Studios, which housed tons of film equipment. His successor, General Park, was a huge fan of Shin and Choi, and he waxed most lyrical about *Evergreen Tree*

(1961), which is set in 1930s Korea. Choi Eun-hee plays the "good teacher," an idealistic character who starts a school in a rural village. Eventually, she overcomes the mistrust of the illiterate villagers and triumphs over Japan's bureaucracy. Children flood into her classroom, and every day she writes her slogan on the chalkboard: "Rouse the masses from darkness!" She joins the farmers in the fields and packs clay on the walls of the school. But she overexerts herself, and her battle with a terminal illness is a drawn-out, melodramatic elegy.

With *Evergreen Tree* in mind, General Park thought Shin should be the man to take over Anyang Studios. The problem was that Shin Films — as his company was now called — would also have to take over Anyang's debts. Shin didn't have much business sense. If one of his films became a blockbuster, he sank all of the profits into his next project, which might flop. Financially speaking, it was a roller coaster. But Shin didn't worry about these things. "Art can't speculate with money," he would say.

Shin also encouraged Madame to direct. In 1965 she made her directorial debut with *A Girl Raised as a Future Daughter-in-Law* (*Minmyeoneuri*), the story of a poor young girl who is sold to a rich family whose rotten son is her intended. At the time, she was only the third-ever female director in South Korea.

When we told Madame that we'd seen this film the other day at Seoul's Korean Film Archive, as well as her subsequent film *Princess in Love* (*Gongjunim-ui jjaksarang*, 1967), she looked surprised. She had no idea that a copy of *Princess in Love* still existed; she thought that it had completely disappeared. In all honesty, she'd never seen the finished film and she would surely be ashamed if she saw it today, she said, and then laughed.

Like so many movies from that time, *Princess in Love* takes places in a historical setting, during the Joseon dynasty. The story follows an Audrey Hepburn-esque princess who falls in love with a man of the people. She tries to escape from the palace in order to get a glimpse of her beloved, who sits by a river and daydreams while fishing. The ruler has his guards secretly follow her. When he discovers she's in love with the young man, the guards capture her and lock her in a cage like a runaway house cat. She is taken back to the palace and "released" back into her golden prison.

In the 1960s, impossible love was a major theme in South Korean films; specifically the power of tradition and the misery that befalls those who try to undermine custom. In both traditional family life and political life, it was disastrous for anyone to cross society's strict boundaries.

BY THE EARLY 1970s, Shin had a shot at becoming the king of South Korean cinema, with Choi as his queen. But Shin and his director colleagues had grown increasingly frustrated by the strict censorship laws, and they began to air their complaints openly. General Park was convinced that Shin was mobilizing the directors guild. When news spread that Shin had also initiated an affair with the young actress Oh Su-mi, the scandal was too much for the dictator. Madame recounted this without bitterness. In 1975, Shin's working permit as a producer was revoked, which meant he was prohibited from working at all. In the same breath, their marriage broke apart.

THE CONDENSATION FROM Madame Choi's glass made a small pool on the marble table. She sat up straight and searched her memory. Maybe she was also searching for the words that would make the unbelievable believable. Finally, she began telling us the story of her kidnapping. How in January 1978 she had turned fifty. How she spent all of her time at the film school that she had started with Shin. How she had travelled to Hong Kong for the business meeting. How the trip was supposed to last no more than ten days, but it would be ten years before she set foot on South Korean soil again.

We had been speaking with Madame Choi for close to three hours. She wasn't showing signs of fatigue, only vague charges of suppressed emotion every now and then. She seemed to have forgotten that the interview was supposed to have lasted only an hour. Now she wanted to take us to lunch.

A taxi was hailed for us, and we sailed into Seoul's viscous traffic. The weather forecasters had predicted that the stormy weather would soon culminate in rain, and their predictions were accurate down to the hour. We had one day left until the rainy season began.

WE WERE LET off on a boulevard lined with sycamores and led into a *bulgogi* restaurant. Steel platters with glowing coals were placed before us. Madame instructed the personnel and soon the table was covered with dishes: two kinds of octopus, two types of kimchi, pepper, garlic in oil, bean paste, and lettuce and perilla leaves to wrap the meat in. Madame ordered several bottles of *soju* and filled our glasses.

She continued telling her story about her time in captivity in the golden palace in North Korea. She talked about her idleness and how she passed the time; how she had longed for her children, worried about her students at the film school, and thought about Shin.

Suddenly, Madame whimpered. She took out a handkerchief and dabbed her eyes behind her large, tinted glasses. She was remembering Shin's appearance at Kim Jong-il's surprise party. She turned to our interpreter and put her fingers between his eyebrows.

"Here were large, white flecks," she said, her voice thick with emotion. "His hair was grey and stood on end. His ankles were completely swollen."

For a moment, Madame sat in silence with her memories. Then she served us our meat, which had finished grilling, and we wrapped it in the leaves. We toasted with our *soju*, but Madame looked sombre. The memories of Shin's hardships had taken hold of her; she said she had a guilty conscience. She had been a luxury-prisoner living in a mansion, and he had suffered the worst.

But once Shin was released and the two were reunited, they were given everything they needed for film production. The resources were unbelievable, and they got to choose their locations in the Soviet Union and China.

"Kim Jong-il was extremely knowledgeable about art and film," said Madame. "He was on the same level as Shin."

We were stunned by her words of praise for her kidnapper, the figure who is always depicted as a mad playboy, ridiculous in his brown creepers, his lifted soles, that chubby body — "North Korea's only fat man" — the applauding baby hands, and above all his hair, that blow-dried swell meant to make him look taller but which actually made him look like an obscure rockabilly artist.

Then we realized that we'd misunderstood an important part of this story. We'd been thinking of it as a Faustian bargain, where the artist-couple chose to sell their souls to those in power. We'd spoken about the princely theme: to be forced to produce, to become an extension of that power. Now Madame was talking about the enormous opportunities they'd been given. For the first time, they didn't have to worry about money. While there was indeed a political agenda, dictated by Kim Jong-il, it had all been very informal when it came to the kidnapped guests. Kim Jong-il loved their films and encouraged them to create.

They hadn't moved from freedom to imprisonment. After all, at the time Korea was made up of two dictatorships. They'd just moved from one prison to the next. And both dictators loved their films.

MADAME WAS FILLING our glasses. Her back was to the large television in the restaurant, so she couldn't see the commercial, which we guessed was for a hair trimmer. A Kim Jong-il lookalike was being filmed from the back, sitting in

180

a barber's chair. The hairdresser had just put the finishing touches to the hair at his neck. "Kim" turned and smiled.

The real Kim Jong-il rearranged the calendar as he saw fit. Shin Sang-ok was born in October, but Kim decided to host a birthday banquet for him in September. In February the next year, they were invited to celebrate Kim Jong-il's birthday. Like Madame's previous invitation to the firstborn son's birthday, this was a sign of being favoured absolutely by the dictator, a favouritism that didn't even extend to members of his innermost political circle. Many were green with envy.

ONE OF THE films Shin and Madame made in North Korea was *Salt* (*Sogeum*, 1985). We'd seen it listed in an anthology about female filmmakers in South Korea as Choi Eun-hee's fourth and final film as a director. But now she denied directing it. She said her name was often added as co-director, but she didn't know why. Shin was the director and Madame had played the lead. At the 1985 Moscow International Film Festival, she was awarded the Best Actress prize for her performance in *Salt*.

The grand international productions were what mattered to the couple because these allowed them to stretch the boundaries of their imprisonment. They were issued passports and could move around the Eastern bloc, even if North Korean "bodyguards" constantly shadowed them. Shin was clever about satisfying the system. He used the KAPF texts, which always had a revolutionary foundation, as a starting point. And then he put his own spin on them.

IN 1986, THE couple was invited to be on the jury at a film festival in Vienna. They were chaperoned by their bodyguards. On the way to the festival's cinema they were given the unusual opportunity of taking their own taxi. Their overcoats were in the taxi behind them. At one point, a couple of cars cut between the two vehicles. Shin and Madame noted this and convinced their driver to turn right at a crossing, in the direction of the American embassy. Soon, the bodyguards realized that they'd been shaken off. They radioed the chauffeur in the couple's car and asked him where they were. At that moment, Shin and Madame handed the driver a bundle of cash and convinced him to lie about where they were going.

The car neared the American embassy, and at last found a place to stop. They threw themselves out of the taxi and rushed onto the grounds of the embassy. Madame and Shin asked for political asylum in the United States. But Madame has never forgotten that Shin pushed past her in order to get through the door of the American embassy first.

OUR LUNCH ENDED with cold glass noodles in large stainless-steel bowls. It was a meal in itself. Glass noodles should be easy to swallow, but they clumped together and slid around our mouths like a second tongue. Madame, on the other hand, hungrily slurped hers up. It had been Shin's favourite dish, she said. He used to empty his bowl with only two lifts of his chopsticks.

Madame continued her story, looking worried as she spoke about Kim Jong-il. The dictator had refused to believe that they had left him out of their own free will. He sent a letter in which he offered to help them get back to Pyongyang. Madame spoke as if she were in his debt. She and Shin made seven films during those eight years and another ten were in development. They had paid back everything that had been put in an Austrian bank account for their services in North Korea. Every dollar. That's probably why she was still alive, she speculated. Otherwise she might have been murdered by North Korean agents.

The staff started to clear the table. Madame stood up and grabbed her handbag. We followed her to the cash register, where she elegantly placed the bill on the counter. It had been taken care of without either of us noticing.

Outside the restaurant we met Madame's son, who was going to take her to the hospital for a regular check-up. The man was in his forties, and he was one of the two children that Madame and Shin had adopted. Shin and his lover, Oh Su-mi, also had two children but Oh died in a car accident in Hawaii and, since then, Madame had looked upon Oh's children as her own.

We said goodbye and slowly started walking back down the sycamore-lined boulevard to the hum of the traffic.

THE NEXT DAY, we took a trip to the old city wall in Seoul and saw traces of shamanistic rituals in the forest. Food had been offered to the forefathers, even though small signs had been posted stating that shamanistic rituals were forbidden.

Shamanism still has sweeping importance in South Korea. Regular citizens and politicians, members of the military, and leaders of business turn to shamans, mediums (*mudang*), and clairvoyants (*jumsung-ga*) for help with important questions, even if they often don't acknowledge it publicly. Many still think it would be irresponsible to not pay a specialist (*chonmunga*) for advice when naming a baby. Destiny is written into a name.

Shamanism has deep roots, deeper than the Confucianism imported from China, and often this more impassioned and unbridled belief system has a stronger impact on daily life. The flashes of hot temper and open superstition you encounter in South Korea are far from the restraint and unflagging integrity of the people in neighbouring Japan. In North Korea, the supernatural powers that the ruling dynasty possesses, according to propaganda, are presumably tied to the shamanistic tradition ingrained in Korea.

AFTER WE WANDERED along the city wall, we sat in a screening room in the film archive and watched *Salt*, the film Madame had told us about the previous day. It's a story about one woman's unrelenting hardships, in the vein of Maxim Gorky's socially engaged melodramas. *Salt* introduced a number of new concepts in North Korean film, Madame had explained. Before, cinema was considered the fruit of the nameless collective's efforts, but with this film the director's and actors' names were listed in the credits. Dialect was used for the first time instead of standardized North Korean, which was a dramatic development. The public was shocked by certain scenes. One rape scene was so explicit that Kim Il-sung himself was forced to publicly defend it, explaining that it was motivated by art.

Salt takes place in the 1930s, when the Japanese colonial rulers and the Chinese landowners made a pact that essentially enslaved all Koreans. Salt was a valuable commodity and is a metaphor for living under oppression. The Koreans live an impoverished life in all respects, "like food without salt." After numerous humiliations and a life of poverty, Madame's character becomes a salt smuggler who gets caught at the Chinese–Korean border. Only in the last scene, when the Communist rebels have killed the Chinese militia group that attacks the smugglers, she understands who the righteous ones are in the political struggle. She realizes that "Communism is the salt of the world." In this way, Shin resolved an ideological problem.

IT WAS REMARKABLE watching Madame play a mother to small children — at the time of filming, she was fifty-seven years old. Even more remarkable was imagining the circumstances of the film's production. Shin had just recovered from his four years of imprisonment on a grass diet, some of it spent in an isolation cell where he couldn't even lie down. Now he was shooting scenes where Madame was thrown in prison, starved, abused, and raped. She plays a victim of social injustice. They themselves were prisoners with a certain amount of artistic freedom and great economic freedom. It was the art itself — their empathy, skills, and vision — that Kim Jong-il coveted. He understood that certain things couldn't be bought with money or created in a laboratory. People with specialized skills and unique talent were simply useful bodies that had to be obtained, and one had to hope that they wouldn't fall to pieces. Maybe those years of imprisonment were meant to give them experiences that they could then channel into art. Perhaps this had been his plan.

* * *

IN A PARKING lot on our way out of Panmunjom in the DMZ, we bump into Alejandro Cao de Benós de Les y Pérez. This complicated name belongs to a thirty-four-year-old Spanish man of noble birth, known for his participation in the documentary *Friends of Kim*. There he was simply called Alejandro, short and sweet. He was, and is, president of the Korean Friendship Association (KFA).

In the documentary, the camera followed his officious progress, travelling around the country and participating in a peaceful march calling for reunification, as well as various "acts of solidarity" with the North Korean people. After the march, members of the KFA join a group of North Korean workers for an hour. As part of this performance, Alejandro carries a pile of stones in solidarity with a labourer and makes a lofty proclamation about North Korea: "We are constructing a paradise, a worker's paradise. And that's the most important thing."

"And how far along are we?" asks the documentarian. "Halfway?"

"Oh, I think more than halfway," Alejandro responds. "If we compare with the rest of the world, we are already at

80 percent. And if we are talking about human feelings and heart, we are at least 95 percent there."

The documentary shows seeds of doubt growing among the KFA members, who become ever more wary of the "wonder" that is North Korea, while Alejandro, unfazed, charges forth, leading group songs and shaking hands with everyone he meets.

In Panmunjom he tries to lead the group in protest against the United States, bellowing: "Yankees go home." Toward the end of the trip he breaks into a room belonging to a journalist in the group, the American Andrew Morse, who was then with ABC News. He pries open a locked box, confiscates video footage and notes, and then hands them over to the authorities. Alejandro forces Morse to sign a confession of guilt, stating that he apologizes for all the criticisms he has voiced during a visit to a farming collective. Only then is he allowed to leave the country.

Since 2000, Alejandro has been responsible for North Korea's official website. The country has been so pleased with his contributions it has awarded him a series of honours, as well a position in the Committee for Cultural Relations with Foreign Countries.

Alejandro looks very happy as he climbs aboard our bus. He wears a well-tailored outfit that he is said to have designed himself, based on the uniform of the Korean People's Army. Elias pushes to the front to get his photo taken with Alejandro, who straightens up and smiles. His military attire has virtually no wrinkles or creases.

When Alejandro has taken his leave and the bus rolls

away from Panmunjom, Ari and Trond take out their North Korean flag and start singing "The Internationale," a popular socialist anthem that has been sung since the late nineteenth century.

The videographer is ready with his camera again.

THE DMZ IS a no man's land that stretches along the two countries' border. It is a wide area that contains green fields and a small village called Kijong-dong, which the South Koreans say is a façade — that the houses are merely cement shells patrolled by functionaries and the lights are turned on and off at regular intervals. Here in the village, the North Koreans have erected one of the world's tallest flagpoles — 160 metres — in order to break the record held by the South Koreans, who built a 98-metre flagpole in the DMZ village Daeseong-dong in the 1980s. They also started an audio war. Since the 1950s, the North Koreans have bombarded the South with revolutionary operas and propaganda speeches using enormous loudspeakers. In 2004, the South retaliated with a sonic wall of Korean pop. This time the two sides managed to end this unbearable situation at the negotiation table, where they agreed to a sonic ceasefire.

Soon after we leave the DMZ, we get a flat tire. Mr. Song, the bus driver, and the videographer are down to their undershirts, struggling to change the tire in the heat. The Bromma boys think it's incredibly funny; Bruno, who towers over everyone like a giant, calmly observes it all. He's about twice as tall as Mr. Song and could easily lift the tire without having to bend his knees. His enormous back and muscles are ready to spring into action. We look expectantly at him. But Mr. Song and the bus driver don't want his help; they are going to take care of this with true Juche spirit, or *"uri minjok-kkiri"* — "only our people together [can take care of this]" — as they say in both North and South Korea.

One of the Bromma boys spreads out a beach towel on the asphalt, strips to his underwear, and lies down. One of his friends takes a picture of him posing. He makes sure to get the tire-changing in the background. Tiny North Koreans struggling with giant tires.

"This is fun," he says.

* * *

SHIN SANG-OK AND Madame Choi weren't alone in their plight as prisoners in North Korea. But what differentiates their destiny from other abductees is that we have a public record of their activities: their movies. The films they made in the North can be seen as documents filled with messages and metaphors. One feature that wasn't made during their time in North Korea, but which has still been endowed with symbolic value, is the 1964 drama *Red Muffler (Ppal-gan mahura)*. This film commemorates the South Korean air raids on the North during the Korean War. Shin had half of the film's 35mm negatives with him when he was kidnapped, as well as *The Red Gate (Yeolnyeomun,* 1962) and *Pyongyang Bombing Squad (Pyongyang pokgyokdae,* 1971). The reels were seized, but Shin managed to record what he had of *Red Muffler* with a video camera. After the couple's escape from North Korea, this was merged with the other half of the film in South Korea. The result is a remarkable document that explores both the division of the country and Shin's own story. We watched the spliced version at the Korean Film Archive in Seoul. The quality of Shin's video footage creates a filter, like a new layer of history in the story of the war.

The film's title plays on the red muffler scarfs the South Korean fighter pilots wore with pride, but which at the same time carried with them the values of the Red Guard and the associations of North Korean schoolchildren. The mufflers synthesize values and worlds, not least establishing a link between North and South, as David Scott Diffrient shows in the essay "Han'guk Heroism: Cinematic Spectacle and the Postwar Cultural Politics of *Red Muffler*." The muffler is a symbol of the enemy's scalp, and an object that saves lives, and something that is passed on from hand to hand in the same way that the character Chi-son, played by Madame Choi, goes from owner to owner, from wife to prostitute to wife again.

General Park gave Shin generous resources for this project: *Red Muffler* was to become a military recruitment film as well as a celebration of the South Korean dictator himself. In the scenes in which North Korean villages are bombed, no maimed people or crying children are shown; instead we are given the pilot's perspective as he looks over the controls and levers, like in a video game.

The scarf in the film is connected to the "fear of the colour red" (or "red complex") — a historical trauma in South

Korea. Ever since the Korean War, the colour had been contaminated with the constant threat of the Communists in the North. People who wore red shirts risked being told off; a red carpet in a hotel room might upset people.

The first step taken toward recontexualizing the colour happened at the 2002 World Cup, when it was appropriated by the Red Devils — the South Korean team's devoted fans — who took over the streets with their red shirts and their drumming and their jubilant cheers.

OUR BUS IS back on Pyongyang's streets and we see members of the Youth Corps everywhere. They march in neat rows, wearing bright red scarves that stand out against their white shirts. From the age of three, children are schooled in ideology. From eight to fourteen, they wear the red scarf. When they turn fourteen, they trade it in for a pin featuring Kim Il-sung's portrait. The scarf is proof of their direct connection to the Kim Il-sung Socialist Youth League.

*   *   *

MOST PEOPLE IN both North and South Korea know the folk tale that the movie *Pulgasari* is based on. But Kim Jong-il wanted to rewrite the story. To understand the meaning behind *Pulgasari*, you have to revisit the original — *Godzilla*. *Gojira*, as it is called in Japanese, is a character born of the nuclear age. The original 1954 movie is neither kitschy nor ironic, even if the special effects wouldn't exactly impress an audience in the digital age. *Godzilla* is often automatically classified as a B-movie, but in fact it was one of the most expensive films ever produced in Japan, with the equivalent of a budget of sixty-five million dollars today. *Godzilla* is a dark, melancholic elegy with deliberate symbology and sophisticated sound design; it is an allegorical film with political content.

The movie opens with a scene of a fishing boat that is annihilated by a beam of light, a reference to an event that happened in March of that year: the Americans testing a 1.5-megaton hydrogen bomb at Bikini Atoll in the Pacific Ocean. The Japanese tuna boat *Lucky Dragon 5* was nearby and was covered in radioactive debris. The crew fell ill with radiation poisoning and the incident, which was called the "tuna scare," set off an international crisis. A fear of radiation poisoning spread throughout Japan once more.

In the film, Godzilla originated in the Jurassic age and has been living at the bottom of the ocean. But when his habitat is destabilized by the Americans' test explosions, the homeless monster absorbs the radiation and begins to wander. The navy deploys depth charges and the military erects a high-voltage wire along the coast. But nothing can touch Godzilla. The monster's carapace glows and a radioactive heat ray shoots from his mouth, melting buildings and houses.

Japanese audiences recognized the references to the recent past in the film's images: for them the smoking ruins of Tokyo the day after Godzilla's rampage were a reminder of the devastating bombing of the city at the end of the war. The images of burned people at the hospital and children being examined with Geiger counters brought up fresh, painful memories of Hiroshima and Nagasaki.

Finally, a naval ship is sent out to sea for the last stand against the monster. The military is using a new super-weapon created by a scientist named Dr. Serizawa, who chooses to die with the monster. The final scenes are devoid of triumph. One doubts that Godzilla is the last of its kind. If the nuclear tests continue, a new Godzilla will rise from the sea.

EIJI TSUBURAYA, the famous special effects master at Toho Studios in Tokyo, was responsible for the look of the Godzilla monster. All of Tsuburaya's characters, including Rodan (the terrifying flying lizard), Mothra (a giant moth), Booska (the predecessors to the Teletubbies), and Ultraman (the humanoid alien in stylish red-and-silver costume), are beloved by the Japanese and have been popularized through film, video games, comic books, TV series, model kits, and toys. Even Tsuburaya himself has been cast as a collectible figure dressed in his signature style: sunglasses, pork pie hat, white shirt buttoned up to his neck, and a pen in his breast pocket. The only thing missing is the eternally burning cigarette.

But none of Tsubaraya's other imaginative figures can ever measure up to Godzilla, "Japan's most famous international film star," memorialized as a national monument that stands in Ginza. *Godzilla* is the most enduring series in film history—twenty-nine films have been made over a period of fifty years.

WHEN TSUBARAYA CREATED the monster, he'd already had a long career as a cinematographer and a director. Toho Studios was created in 1936 by Ichizo Kobayashi — a railroad magnate, politician, and bigwig in the entertainment world — and Tsuburaya was hired one year later. During the war, Tsuburaya was summoned to the Imperial Japanese Navy Air Service. His assignment was to make instructional films for fighter pilots, and he himself became a skilled aerobatic pilot. The attack on Pearl Harbor had unleashed a euphoric wave of nationalism, and it was thought that a big film about the honourable blitz would convince the Japanese people that total victory was nigh.

Five months after the attack, Tsuburaya began working on an incredibly advanced reconstruction of the events for the film. Using photographs supplied by the navy as reference, he built a detailed, grand-scale model of Pearl Harbor in the backlot of Toho Studios, recreating the destruction: the American battleships set alight by bombs and the spread of black smoke over the harbour.

After this, Toho became drawn farther into the military's propaganda machine, to the point where their operations merged. The worse the war went for Japan, the greater Toho's mission. Near the end, they were even given access to fighter planes fresh from the factory. In desperation, the studio created pompous, heroic films that deviated ever more from reality.

After the war ended, the Americans found the film stock featuring Tsuburaya's sophisticated set design. They thought they were looking at actual footage of the attack. Some scenes were even incorporated into their own documentaries about Pearl Harbor. Tsuburaya's special effects were so advanced that the Americans made sure he was fired from Toho Studios. Considering his detailed knowledge about the geography of Pearl Harbor, they concluded he must have been a spy during the war.

After a few years Tsuburaya returned to Toho Studios, but initially he was forced to operate incognito. After the American occupation officially ended in 1952, his name could once again be listed in the film credits. When work started on *Godzilla* he was resurrected as a special effects specialist.

Tsuburaya put an extraordinary amount of energy into making sure everything in the film was perfect. The Tokyo that he created for the movie was to 1/25 scale, and the buildings had complete interiors so that they would collapse realistically. Tsuburaya wasn't happy with his first model, so after "Tokyo" was destroyed by the monster, everything had to be rebuilt from scratch.

The pioneering actor who was given the illustrious job of bringing the monster to life was Haruo Nakajima. He lost twenty-two pounds during the shoot of the first film — after every take they poured his sweat out of the costume. Nakajima pulled on that rubber suit for eighteen years, from 1954 until 1972. He fainted numerous times from the poisonous fumes of burning kerosene-soaked rags. Once he was nearly electrocuted, and another time an avalanche of crushed ice fell on him, to name just a few of his hardships. Like Tsuburaya, Nakajima embodied the Japanese culture of duty. When a person is given a task, he takes that task seriously, burrowing deeper and deeper into his obligations. The years pass by and he faithfully goes to the office until the day he retires. The monotony seems to have polished him until he sparkles, and it is this sparkle that he leaves behind.

Nakajima's successor was Kenpachiro Satsuma. The former steelworker, whose actual name was Kengo Nakayama, began his monster career playing Hedorah (the Smog Monster) in *Godzilla vs. Hedorah*. Satsuma was never given any speaking parts because of his rustic Kyushu accent. In 1984, when Toho was planning on making a lavish new remake of the original *Godzilla*, Satsuma was given the honour of wearing the 265-pound costume. Through horseback riding, karate, and judo, he kept trim and was able to keep it on for ten minutes at a time. Previous stuntmen had fainted after two. Satsuma would be faithful to the rubber suit until 1995. He arrived at the *Pulgasari* shoot in North Korea straight from the set of Toho's *Godzilla* remake.

* * *

THE BUS DROPS us off at the Koryo Hotel, which is supposed to be the most luxurious tourist hotel in Pyongyang. Our group is worn out after the long trip back from Kaesong. The Värmlanders, Ari, Bruno, Trond, Andrei, the fighter pilot, and the others take a seat in the lobby. The tattooed baker has a stomach ache. He hasn't been able to go to the bathroom for a whole week. We and the Bromma boys take the elevator up to the panoramic bar on the forty-fourth floor. Elias and Oksana tag along, too.

Oksana is indefatigable, but Elias is no longer enthusiastic. He is shrouded in disillusionment and fatigue. At the start of the trip, he spoke of finding work in Pyongyang as an interpreter or at the Swedish embassy. Now he says he's given up on those plans. This country is far too crazy, he says. It was worse than he could ever have imagined. And it has been impossible to make contact with a single regular North Korean.

We are the only guests in the bar. Photography is strictly forbidden. The view is of the Forbidden City, the walled part of Pyongyang where only the highest echelon of the elite live. Within these walls are four luxurious multi-family complexes, and stores with goods that no one else can afford to buy.

In the mid-1980s, the Russian author and North Korea expert Andrei Lankov studied in Pyongyang and wrote one of the few existing pieces of reportage about daily life in North Korea. He became interested in this particular neighbourhood and observed the youths that sometimes walked out from behind its walls: "They wore impressive clothing or Kim Jong-il suits. Their faces radiated contempt for those who were inferior to them, the poor and malnourished. Even the obligatory Kim Il-sung badge was worn as a fashion statement. The children of nobility wore the badge highest up on their lapels."

This is where the families in the party's upper echelon live. The Bromma boys come up with ruses to distract the wait staff so we can take a picture of the area. But what does this part of town say about Pyongyang? Which world capitals don't have exclusive, walled-in neighbourhoods, and most far more extensive than this one? There is much that is upsetting and grotesque in North Korea, but faced with the Forbidden City, it's hard to work up any ire. During our trip we've seen the same contempt in our own group that Lankov saw in the faces of the youth as they walked out of their sheltered world.

*   *   *

GODZILLA'S SUCCESS IN Japan created a new genre, the *kaiju* movie, or monster movie, which quickly spread to neighbouring countries. In 1962, the South Korean film director Kim Myeong-je contributed the first version of *Pulgasari* to the genre. The film itself was lost, but two movie posters surfaced in later years, proof that it did in fact exist. The story was based on the same Korean folk tale as Shin Sang-ok's *Pulgasari*, but in this earlier version a martial arts master is murdered and reborn as iron-eating monster.

Shin Sang-ok's version opens on a blue-hued studio environment that's supposed to depict a settlement in the 1300s, during the Koryo dynasty. The villagers live simple and virtuous lives. The men don't need to adhere to the five hairstyles that are on offer today; instead, they sport black manes with headbands, and they fill in their eyebrows and wear mascara. They are reminiscent of how Native Americans are represented in John Ford films. The women move demurely, wearing traditional, pastel-coloured *hanbok*s.

The village smith has been thrown in jail after the

discovery of a stockpile of iron tools that he was hiding from the feudal lord's army, which was collecting all metal to be forged into weapons. Before he dies in prison, he makes a small figure out of rice. His daughter finds it among his garments and takes it home as a memento. Consumed with sorrow, the heroine absentmindedly pricks her finger with a needle while she's sewing. A drop of blood lands on the rice figure, which she keeps in her sewing box. But she doesn't notice the burst of red light that emanates from the model at this life-giving moment.

The figurine springs to life, stands, grabs a needle, and gobbles it up. When it finishes all the needles, it takes a giant leap and lands in the girl's arms so it can devour the needle she's holding.

Pulgasari grows rapidly, and soon joins the villagers in a revolt against the feudal king and finally storms the imperial palace. But the monster becomes far too demanding. Its insatiable appetite for iron makes it increasingly difficult to keep Pulgasari satisfied. The heroine martyrs herself in order to annihilate the beast.

It is understood that Shin Sang-ok had great difficulty working with the special effects department to try and make Pulgasari look like a giant. One solution was to take close-ups of the monster's feet, of which he had large-scale models built. When Pulgasari's full size is revealed, Shin inset a flickering, blue-toned projection of the monster that the actors moved in front of.

Shin spared no expense for the final battle scene, employing thousands of extras and creating real explosions that made earth rain over the actors on the battlefield. The revolutionary message is underscored by the rebels' red banners. Enormous cannons with muzzles cast in the shape of dragons' mouths are fired from the palisades of the imperial palace. Pulgasari catches the cannonballs in his mouth as if they were breath mints and spits them back out so the palisades crumble.

Pulgasari's ability to deflect any attacker's assaults is a reference to Godzilla's radioactive heat ray, which incinerates houses and cars. When Pulgasari is let loose on the imperial palace in slow motion, it's clear that the two monsters are cut from the same cloth, not just because Kenpachiro Satsuma is the actor inside both costumes, but also in the choreography and lust for destruction.

YOU COULD SAY that Shin's *Pulgasari* is a criticism of Kim Jong-il's power over the people, that the emperor symbolizes the despot who lives a life of luxury while the people are crippled by hardship. In one important scene, women collect bark from the trees in order to add filler to their diet, foreshadowing the poor harvest and famine. But this critical perspective is unthinkable in North Korea. The heroine is the Mother of Joseon, the united Korea. The oppressors are the capitalists in the South, or alternatively Japan, or the United States. The fight is against them. And the nuclear warheads should be pointed at them. The weapon is created internally, with earth, rice, and blood. Its nourishment — iron that has been enriched in the forge — represents uranium. The weapon is transformed and refined so that it possesses even greater devilish power. In the end, only the spirit of the people can disarm the weapon. But it's not a total disarmament. One spawn is born, and carries with it the potential to grow and come to the aid of the North Korean people when it is needed.

A WELL-KNOWN METHOD of unifying people is the demonization of others. In South Korea, schoolchildren were taught that Kim Il-sung had horns growing out of his forehead. On children's television programs, North Korean leaders were depicted as wolves that drained their countrymen of blood. On North Korean propaganda posters, Americans are depicted with claws and paws. An oft-repeated epithet is that Americans are "monsters."

Monsters are used to create fear and a physical boundary that you have to be careful not to cross. The feral part of the creature represents the impossibility of integration. But it takes a monster to fight a monster. Like your enemy, you too enter into a pact with a beast that will come to your aid if needed, and so the monstrous machinery of war is created.

North Korea's nuclear weapons program was created at the exact same time as *Pulgasari*. In 1985, the country completed construction on its first nuclear weapons facility and, though the program wasn't officially acknowledged, the film was Kim Jong-il's acknowledgement in parable form. Twenty-one years later, in 2006, the nuclear weapons test was a fresh, unequivocal acknowledgement. The monster had long been fed in Kilju's underworld, and now he took the opportunity to display his power.

* * *

SOME OF US in the group are going to see a second performance at the 1st of May Stadium, a mass gymnastics recital. This time we smuggle our video camera in.

The same wall of schoolchildren take their places in the stands, holding their colourful sheets of paper. The children have learned to focus all of their attention on one single person, a director who uses numbers and command flags. Everything is about synchronization. The goal is to become one with the masses, to work as one single organism; only then can you create the world's largest show.

The rehearsals are as important as the recital itself. By drilling in the movement pattern and coordinating their bodies with the other players over the years, each individual is disciplined to be part of the collective movement. B. R. Myers asserts that conformity is a tribute to racial purity: "These games are not the grim Stalinist exercises in anti-individualism that foreigners . . . often misperceive them as, but joyous celebrations of the pure-bloodedness and homogeneity from which the race's superiority derives."

With lightning speed, a gigantic landscape materializes that makes us gasp: a mountain wrapped in the night's mist, with the sea in the background. The red glow of the sinking sun casts orange and violet reflections on the sharp peaks. In the foreground, raw emeralds and chrysanthemums appear without shattering the illusion. In a flash, the scene is gone. A new picture unfolds and the field is flooded with thousands of schoolgirls in red dresses with hula hoops.

When we watch the footage afterwards, we discover small deviations in what had seemed like perfectly synchronized movements. The camera has caught details that the naked eye couldn't possibly detect in the enormous stadium. One girl loses her rhythm; another misses a step while jumping rope. The rope gets caught around her waist and she looks hopelessly alone in the masses.

* * *

AFTER A MEAL of duck and *soju* at a local restaurant — a standard farewell meal for all tourist groups in Pyongyang — we are driven back to the hotel. The Bromma boys aren't with us. They've long been talking about their dinner with the Swedish ambassador, and tonight's the night. But the Värmlanders don't seem to miss them; neither does anyone else in the group, for that matter.

On the ride back to the hotel, we all begin to get into a Friday-night kind of mood. Trond and Ari are on fire. They are moving up and down the aisle like Laurel and Hardy. A mist of *soju* rises up toward the ceiling. The Värmlanders are downing beers with the fighter pilot; Oksana's cheeks are rosy.

At the front of the bus, Mr. Song holds the microphone and tenderly sings one of his favourite songs, Elton John's "Candle in the Wind." His job is almost done and no one has caused too much trouble. Ms. Kim looks happy. In honour of our last night in North Korea, she wears a white *joseonot*.

For the whole trip, we have been fawning over Mr. Song and Ms. Kim. We aren't risking anything by challenging the rules and sneaking off on our own. Tourists who are suspected of being CIA agents might be taken into custody and interrogated for a few hours, but a guide who hasn't kept his tourists in line can end up in a camp.

THE PARTY WILL continue at the panoramic restaurant at the Yanggakdo Hotel. But first, we're invited into a room off the lobby to watch *The Movie of Our Trip*. The cameraman has hastily cut the material together and added an intolerable synthesizer soundtrack. The film begins with pre-recorded sequences of happy children running in the grass. Then scene after scene unfolds of our visits to various monuments. We quickly grow bored and the group disperses.

In the elevator we bump into one of Nils's acquaintances: a tall, blond Estonian man with horn-rimmed glasses wearing a turquoise polo shirt. Nils had hardly expected to run into friends or acquaintances in an elevator at the Yanggakdo Hotel in Pyongyang, but the Estonian doesn't seem to think it's at all strange. The man has a Russian passport and has lived most of his life in Siberia. Now he lives in Tallinn, where he is making a killing as an importer of exclusive Italian coffee and exotic types of tea. He spends his money on trips to places like Malawi, Kiribati, and North Korea. The Estonian possesses a strange calm, a near-enlightened glow. The world is his oyster. Through his horn-rimmed glasses he can calmly observe what's going on in the shadowy corners of the world.

UP IN THE bar, we find the Bromma boys seated at a table with the Swedish ambassador, who is pale and dressed in a dark grey suit that is slightly too big for him. The dinner at the embassy didn't happen. They'll have to satisfy themselves with a Taedong beer. Sitting up as straight as Sunday school students, they listen while the ambassador holds court.

Sweden was one of the first countries to set up an embassy in Pyongyang. In 1975, Erik Cornell opened the embassy, which for twenty years was the only consulate for all Westerners in North Korea. Others haven't been as successful. The diplomats at the Australian embassy, which opened the same year as the Swedish one, were given forty-eight hours to pack up and leave after a toga party. That was the straw that broke the camel's back for the North Koreans, who were unhappy with their approach to diplomacy and behaviour from the start. The Australians were in Pyongyang for only six months. They had thought that they, in typical diplomatic fashion, could negotiate and come to a compromise, and they had also asked to visit prisons and courts. This kind of behaviour was unacceptable to the North Korean government. The Swedish embassy has avoided becoming the annoyance that Australia's was by taking a soft and accommodating line. They believe that submissive contact is better than no contact at all.

There is no normal diplomatic life in Pyongyang, says Cornell in *North Korea under Communism: Report of an Envoy to Paradise*. The North Korean military has built tunnels under embassy buildings so that they can enter them through holes in the floor. At the Swedish embassy, local employees are chosen by the North Korean state. During Cornell's time, the housekeeper was most likely an intelligence officer. Once, when she was serving at a formal dinner party, they heard the crackling sound of audio surveillance equipment under her *joseonot*.

Cornell describes how the staff at the embassy were not allowed any contact with regular Koreans. Even the ambassadors from Communist countries were not permitted to engage in any form of intellectual exchange with the citizens. During a banquet, the wife of the Cuban ambassador tried to discuss North Korean burial customs with a female senior official in the North Korean administration, Cornell writes. She had noticed that there were no burial grounds in Pyongyang. When she asked about it, the official replied seriously: "You understand, here in the Democratic People's Republic of Korea people do not die so much."

WE SIT DOWN at a table that Trond has already filled with beer bottles. But Trond can't sit still. He goes over to the ambassador's table and circles it like a drugged circus bear. He slaps one of the Bromma boys on the back, and shoves his business card under the ambassador's nose. The Bromma boys' gazes wander. This isn't how they imagined their last night in Pyongyang. The trip to this bizarre country was supposed to have been crowned with an invitation to supper in a magnificent dining room in the embassy.

BRUNO SITS CLOSEST to the window at our table. He hasn't shaved and he looks worn out. He is tired of his job in

Beijing and he's tired of being single. His business manufactures precision instruments for medical use. It's hard for us to reconcile the image of his large mass with a precision scale that can measure a thousandth of a gram.

Bruno wants to move on. He wants to get a better job in the United States, but he says it's impossible if you've been caught on camera bowing to a Kim Il-sung statue. He's slouching and looks regretful.

"But I didn't bow," he says in his Schwarzenegger accent. "No, I didn't bow."

He seems to have forgotten where he is; he's mostly talking to himself. He looks out into the darkness: "No, I didn't bow."

We don't want to say that we have just seen him bow to a Kim Il-sung statue in the *The Movie of Our Trip*.

* * *

AT HIS OCTOBER 2007 meeting in Pyongyang with South Korea's President Roh Moo-hyun, Kim Jong-il flattered his enemy and acknowledged his desires. President Roh handed over 150 DVDs to add to Kim's cherished collection, among them popular films and South Korean TV series.

Shin Sang-ok said in an interview with the *Guardian* in 2003 that Kim Jong-il preferred action films, "sex films," and horror films. His favourites were Hong Kong action films, James Bond movies, and *Friday the 13th*. Shin said that Kim Jong-il generally considered all movies to be a reflection of reality. "I had to explain to him that most American films were fictional."

Kim Jong-il is often openly mocked about his film fanaticism in newspapers and magazines. We are painted a picture of a giant baby who appears in his own infantile cinematic fantasies. To the dictator, a lightsaber and a Scud missile fall into the same category. His gluttony for film goes hand in hand with his decadence, his cognac, and his food orgies.

But you can also turn it around and see Kim Jong-il as a leader who fully understands the political and mythmaking power of film. For the Third Reich and the Soviet Union, propaganda wasn't hollow; it was a comprehensive reality for the people.

North Korea's leader has learned that film has the power to simultaneously create, mirror, and reshape the national identity and mentality. The Second World War's victors mirrored themselves in heroic self-representation, while the war's losers made films that broke with tradition — films that helped these nations work through the trauma as they tried to piece together the shards of their shattered identities — Italian neorealism and Japanese monster movies, for example. Shin Sang-ok's melodramas may have served this purpose in South Korea in the 1950s.

IN *OUR ESCAPE HAS NOT YET ENDED* — the book that the film couple published in 2001 — Shin says, just as Madame did during our conversation, that you have to take the dictator's film knowledge seriously. According to Shin, Kim Jong-il is also an authority on music. The leader can easily identify which instrument in a symphony orchestra is playing off-key.

The book also gives a detailed account of the function of the North Korean film archive. The archive is kept in a building, like a super-brain or a motherboard. Located behind massive steel fences in the heart of Pyongyang, the structure is climate-controlled, fully maintained, and guarded by 250 employees. The symbolism couldn't be more potent.

SHIN AND MADAME were first introduced to the archive on March 14, 1983. The three-storey building may be the largest film repository in the world. Voice actors, translators, subtitle specialists, projectionists and recording specialists, in addition to security and other types of workers, are employed here. All the North Korean films that have ever been made are stored in a special room.

Later, when Shin and Madame were given free access to the collection, Shin made a discovery: he found the missing negatives of the first version of the *Shim Cheong* myth from 1972. He had sent it to Kim Guh-wha at Shin Films in Hong Kong so it could be subtitled in Chinese. It was clear that the same man who had sent these negatives to Kim Jong-il had also lured Madame into the trap.

During our conversation, Madame had mentioned an audio recording of an hours-long monologue that Kim Jong-il had delivered in October 1983. Madame, taking a great risk, had secretly recorded forty-five minutes of it. Military intelligence services consider her recording to be one of the leading sources in revealing the dictator's psychological make-up. It speaks volumes about how Kim Jong-il views the role of culture in winning over the masses:

We send our people to East Germany to study editing, to Czechoslovakia to study camera technology, and to the Soviet Union to learn directing. Other than that, we cannot send our people to go anywhere since they are enemy states. No France, no West Germany, no Great Britain. We especially have to have conduct exchange with Japan, but we cannot even allow [North Korean] people to watch Japanese films. We end up analyzing foreign films to imitate them but there is a limit to what we can do, but our efforts have brought no progress. I have been struggling with this problem for five years [since 1978]. All we ended up doing was to send a couple of people to the Soviet Union after the liberation and to establish a Film Institute, but they are not that impressive after all. I acknowledge that we lag behind in filmmaking techniques. We have to know that we are lagging behind and make efforts to raise a new generation of filmmakers.

Considering Juche Thought's emphasis on self-reliance, it may seem illogical to kidnap people from the outside world simply because you need them. But perhaps the need for specialized skills was greater than the Juche ideal of self-reliance.

As the head of cinematic arts, Kim Jong-il had decided to make a concerted effort to liven up North Korean film. His obedient workers in the state film industry knew the appropriate topics to cover and that cinema was a tool for political education. But their productions were mind-numbingly dull. Shin Sang-ok was a star who had fallen out of favour, and Madame Choi was a legend. He needed their raw talent to gild his existence and to get the art of cinema back on its feet. Above all, it seems that Kim Jong-il was searching for the key to melodrama. He felt that if you perfected the art of the melodrama, then you could engage people's emotions. This was the crucial secret ingredient that would elevate North Korean propaganda.

DAY 8

LITTLE BOY

T HE CODE NAME for the bomb dropped on Hiroshima was "Little Boy." When the artist Takashi Murakami gave the same name to his 2005 exhibition about post-war aesthetics in Japan, he wanted to shed light on a national trauma. The Americans dropped two atomic bombs. Japan lost the war and ties to its ancient samurai traditions were cut. According to Murakami the bomb castrated the Japanese men and infantilized the country. The Japanese post-war constitution was a carbon copy of America's, with one exception: the unique Article 9, stipulating that Japan would never arm itself again. Japan's fate was sealed, and what followed was the nation's descent into a world of cute. Japan became *kawaii* (the Japanese word for cuteness) and Japanese men became "Little Boys."

The poster for *Little Boy* depicts a decorative, flattened mushroom-cloud shape that melds the atomic bomb with the plasticity of the cartoon character Barbapapa. The exhibition was a symphony of pop-culture objects and images from the *otaku*-king's kingdom: *kawaii* objects, monster movies, anime, manga, and art. With Godzilla's direct link to the bomb, the monster was featured prominently. "*Otaku*" is the name that was given to a group of Japanese people who, during the economic bubble of the 1980s, turned their back on society and instead obsessed over their hobbies: collecting dolls, model-building, reading manga, and full-time idol worship.

Takashi Murakami's approach can be compared to Andy Warhol's. He doesn't add anything to the culture; instead, he copies it, blows it up in scale, and increases its value. He endows it with clarity and highlights its sorrows and its pains. Of his Mickey Mouse–like character, Mr. DOB, Murakami says: "He is cute but has no meaning and understands nothing of life, sex, or reality." Murakami leaves the true meaning of cuteness open to interpretation — is it about camouflage, working through a trauma, or an embodiment of helplessness? And in that case, who is helpless: the stuffed animal or those who worship it?

YOU COULD SAY that Kim Jong-il is a super-*otaku*, a nerd who has unlimited resources to stage his own passions. You could also say that he created his own interpretation of the neo-liberal term "soft power." Soft power, a concept developed by the American political scientist Joseph Nye, refers to a country's ability to assert its influence not by military force or with economic strength, but with its ability to create an attractive culture. In soft power, pop culture is used to disseminate hidden political messages on a meta-level.

For the past ten years, soft power has risen to become one of the most important economic and political means of persuasion in Japan, and Takashi Murakami has been its prophet. "Cute" in today's Tokyo is all-encompassing. The term "*kawaii*" has become a pop-culture buzzword, but it also manifests across the city: in advertisements, clothes, costumes, accessories, signs, vehicles, and architecture. The streets are filled with the sound of teenage girls calling out "*Kawaii!*" The Asahi Bank features Hello Kitty's predecessor Miffy on its ATMs; Monchhichis, stuffed toy monkeys, adorn packets of condoms; Nippon Airways paid one million dollars to license the famous Pokémon characters in order to plaster them on a few of their Boeing aircraft. On signs advertising the Japanese army — the army that is officially called the Japan Self-Defense Forces — soldiers are depicted as cute action figures.

THROUGHOUT HIS ENTIRE career, Kim Jong-il has loved illusion, drama, and performance. The more lavish the better. His people are schooled in theatrics, which also seep into their daily lives. Through song, gestures, and costume they embody the utopian nation every day. But by 1978 the leader wanted to reach new heights. For this, he needed melodrama.

Kim Jong-il was clearly dissatisfied with his country's attempts at the genre so far. In a conversation recounted by Shin Sang-ok, he complained about North Korean film:

"[The] works have the same expressions, redundancies, the same old plots. All our movies are filled with crying and sobbing. I didn't order them to portray that kind of thing." He wanted real melodrama, not just buckets of tears.

Threats instil fear in a populace. But the threat of an uprising is ever present. Maybe the dictator wanted to complement his harsh methods with softness as a way of winning the hearts of his citizens. Clearly, he had demonstrated an intuitive understanding of soft power when he called for his people to engage in the delicate business of kidnapping Choi Eun-hee and Shin Sang-ok. He seemed to have won over the now hyper-disciplined bodies of the citizens, bodies that took part in parades and performed synchronized gymnastics, all in a neat row. But by making use of the beautiful, the cute, the comic, and the dramatic, he penetrated their inner lives too.

* * *

IN THE 1980s, Kim Jong-il often travelled in his armoured train to cities in North Korea and the Soviet Union. But on several occasions he also took the boat to Tokyo, presumably to secretly watch Hikita Tenko's magic shows at the Cordon Bleu show pub in Akasaka.

As a young singer in the mid-1970s, Mariko Itakura had inherited a famous male magician's act. Oddly enough, she also took over his name and his debts and transformed the act into a great success. Part alien and part anime queen, she delivered hi-tech acts in nightclubs in Macao, featuring lasers and flying unicorns. With her waist-length black hair and wearing a tight red dress, she performed a water tank escape act. She turned her business into a minor empire with its own TV series, perfume, wine, and fashion collections.

Hikita Tenko is the name of one of her two alter egos, and was the name she inherited along with the act. As a character, Hikita is shy and doesn't say much. She is forced to work hard during the performance — nothing comes for free — and she reacts to pulling off her escape act with a vague sense of surprise. Japanese men like cute women, women who need to be protected, and they feel threatened by strong ones. But her other character, Princess Tenko, who performs outside of Japan, is powerful and determined. She is an eternally young heroine.

Every year, Princess Tenko announces that she is twenty-four years old. She says that she wants to live up to the Princess Tenko figures sold by Barbie-manufacturer Mattel, Inc. So, like a doll, she can't change her hair, age, or appearance. So far, she has managed to maintain her doll-like appearance. But of course this isn't sustainable in the long term. So, who knows, perhaps in the future she will be replaced by another Hikita Tenko — whether male or female.

IN A 2007 interview in the *Japan Times*, Hikita Tenko revealed what had happened during the trips she made to North Korea.

In 1988, she visited Pyongyang to perform at the Spring Friendship Art Festival. She discovered that the city was in the process of building a special Princess Tenko theatre.

Her hosts suggested that it would be best for her to settle in Pyongyang.

But she didn't have any plans to move to North Korea. She was Japan's most famous illusionist and performed across the globe, and she spent long periods of time in the United States. In 1994, 165,000 people saw her shows at Radio City Music Hall in New York City.

After some discussion, she was allowed to go back to Japan, on the condition that she would return in a few months. Tenko didn't want to go back to North Korea, but she was subjected to an intense campaign of persuasion. Mysterious things happened in her home. A highly collectible Mickey Mouse figurine was stolen from her car. After a while, she found it in her apartment. Then her family was put under pressure, and in 2000 she finally gave in and decided to return to Pyongyang, where she performed for Kim Jong-il and was invited to his palace.

"What did you talk about with Kim Jong-il?" asked the reporter for the *Japan Times.*

"Well, about the world of entertainment and about illusion...but also ordinary things," Tenko replied.

She was given a snowy-white Pungsan, an ancient and rare breed of North Korean hunting dog. The two other puppies from the litter were given to South Korea's then-president, Kim Dae-jung, during his historic visit with Kim Jong-il in June of that same year.

What did he see in Princess Tenko? Was he entranced by her extravagant aesthetic? Or did it have something to do with the act of illusion itself—the ability to defy the laws of physics and turn fantasy into reality? Were the magic acts more real and more convincing than film? Maybe it had something to do with her eternal youth and beauty, or the mysterious assumption of identities throughout her career? Hikita Tenko seemed to have mastered the art of creating an image of herself, and then imitating that same image.

After her meeting with the North Korean leader, Tenko was informed that it had been decided that she would move to Pyongyang. An excellent solution for all, it was agreed. Everything had been arranged to the highest standard: she was going to be given a beautiful house with domestic staff; a theatre that was specially equipped for grand illusions had been built for her. But Princess Tenko didn't want to be the singing nightingale trapped in the emperor's palace. She protested, but felt powerless. Soon she fell ill. North Korean doctors furnished her with medicine that made her even weaker. The German doctor Norbert Vollertsen paid her a series of visits at the hospital. He was working for the German relief organization Cap Anamur in North Korea and would later write a report about the terrible living conditions in the countryside. During one visit, Vollersten advised her to stop taking her medicine. But the North Korean doctors flew into a rage and forced the German to leave the room.

Hikita Tenko spent one month in the hospital in Pyong-yang before she was on her feet again. She explained to the guards that she had to travel to the United States to record the final voiceover for the animated *Princess Tenko* series. For this, she was irreplaceable. She swore that she would return immediately. Princess Tenko slipped out of Kim Jong-il's cage and flew home to Japan. There, she was assigned a police escort. The Japanese secret service wanted to know every detail about her visit with Kim Jong-il.

* * *

CUTENESS AND FEAR. There's an important similarity between *Godzilla* and *Pulgasari*: the ambiguous treatment of fear as a theme. In both films, the monsters are expected to be terrifying: they are harbingers of destruction, they run wild, and they can eradicate all things human. But they also have another, palliative side. By the 1960s movies, the Japanese Godzilla monster was furnished with far fewer teeth. Its eyes were bigger and its mouth was turned up into something of a smile. The costume was rounded out to give a softer impression, and the monster's battles were inspired by wrestling matches and animated series. The wrestling star Rikidōzan was incredibly popular at the time and the fights were modelled on his matches. When *Monster Zero* was being shot in 1965, the film crew protested Godzilla's victory dance after it knocks out the terrifying three-headed lizard King Ghidorah. It was far too ridiculous, they said. But Tsuburaya insisted the dance would make the children happy.

In *Pulgasari*, Shin stressed this ambivalence between fear and cuteness by portraying the monster as a playful and, frankly, cute character. As a baby, Pulgasari is an animated doll with playful eyes. In one scene, the monster jokes around with the heroine and her brother, and they laugh delightedly at its hijinks.

IN THE PERIOD after Shin Sang-ok escaped from North Korea, the monster's journey into cuteness reached its final destination. In 1986, Shin and Madame were given U.S. residency permits. They had the opportunity to withdraw from the spotlight and live out their days quietly, but Shin wasn't made for sipping ice tea under an umbrella. In the coming years, Shin was hired to direct *3 Ninjas Knuckle Up*, the third film in a series of American children's movies, and he was also made an executive producer on *3 Ninjas Kick Back* and *3 Ninjas: High Noon at Mega Mountain*.

In 1996, he wrote the script for *Galgameth*, a benign fantasy film. The film was released without fanfare and went straight to video, ending up among the rows of other neglected VHS tapes in the children's section of video stores. But those who know the film's backstory understand its value. *Galgameth* is the last branch of the monster family tree that began with *Godzilla* in Japan, continued with *Pulgasari* in North Korea, and ended there in Hollywood. And it was Shin Sang-ok who was responsible for this fantastic arc.

Most of the film was shot in a castle in Romania. In contrast to *Pulgasari*, the production is virtually flawless. The story follows a little prince who wakes up sad. The king is dead. The prince has cried himself to sleep, still shielded from the grim knowledge that his father didn't die of natural causes. The power-hungry black knight, El El, poisoned him and is preparing to usurp the throne. But before the beloved father died, he presented his son with a valuable gift: a small stone sculpture of a strange creature. He called it Galgameth. When the prince's tears land on the sculpture something happens and, during the night, the figure is cloaked in a cloud of stardust.

In the light of dawn, the prince discovers something moving under his blanket. A little lizard-like creature is there, looking at him with round, playful eyes. The prince regards the monster with surprise. The creature leaps onto the chandelier and sinks its teeth in: the monster has an appetite for iron. It doesn't take long for the creature to grow several times its original size. Neither sword nor lance can pierce his armour-like body. Galgameth leads the charge against the black knight. The people are victorious, but the monster has to sacrifice itself for the cause. All monsters must die.

AFTER YEARS IN a work camp and then being forced to make films in North Korea, it's almost incomprehensible that the director would choose to recreate the creative visions of his prison warden. Was he diminishing cruelty by embracing childishness and cuteness?

During a visit to Tokyo in 2006, we contacted *Godzilla* actor Kenpachiro Satsuma's agent and found out that in the mid-1990s Shin had made inquiries as to whether Satsuma would consider wearing the Galgameth costume. Kenpachiro politely declined.

Perhaps Shin had a vision — the same actor in three different monster suits representing three political systems.

* * *

IT IS THE morning of our last day in North Korea. The bus takes us to the train station and we are guided to the platform, past the queueing North Koreans, who have to present their travel documents before they are let through. Masses of people are on the go. For the first time, we find ourselves among regular citizens. A tense and overwrought mood pervades the station. Travelling isn't part of daily life; you have to have a special permit.

Mr. Song and Ms. Kim manage to get us on a Chinese train to Beijing. The train's cars are comfortable. The guides look relieved; they have completed their assignment. They say farewell and everyone in the group shakes their hands. Mr. Song jokes and laughs, then he and Ms. Kim plod off.

We take this rare opportunity to see more of the station and film the crowd. When we raise our camera, people look at us suspiciously and with hostility. Suddenly, Mr. Song leaps out from the shadows. "What are you doing?" he asks sharply. He gives us a disappointed look that says: *What opportunists!*

Mr. Song and Ms. Kim escort us back to our train car and wait until we roll out of the station. Ms. Kim waves and smiles inscrutably; she is wearing her pink dress. Mr. Song isn't smiling, but he's raised his hand somewhere in between the signal to stop and a farewell.

WE ROLL SLOWLY through Pyongyang's suburbs. It's unclear where the countryside begins. We see railway workers covered in soot fixing the tracks; women washing clothes in a ditch. Houses out here are in worse condition than in

Pyongyang. The plaster is flaking off the walls and they're not being maintained. We pass by rice paddies and corn-fields. Little egrets stand still as statues, watching for frogs. Farmers stack newly harvested corn on tarps. This is our eighth day in the country and in a few hours we'll be crossing over the border to China. We can hardly say that we've come to understand what life is like here. We know that everything they eat is grown here, that essentially all their tools are manufactured here, and the work is done by hand. On a good day, they have a domestic beer after a long day's work and then sleep under a Vinalon blanket. Kim Il-sung is the light in their isolated solar system. Their history is passed down with his radiance. Anything that threatens to overshadow this radiance must be eradicated. No acts of heroism, other than his, are possible.

But what is *really* going on in the minds of the people living in this country?

We didn't think we'd find an answer to this question during our trip, but the question is always on our minds.

Twenty-four million people live in North Korea. They live completely different lives, depending on where they are in the social hierarchy, and they live in different realities and think different thoughts. They are not robots. For many, life must be a daily struggle for survival. Not just for those in the work camps, but also those in isolated rural areas that don't have access to relief consignments because they are the people who belong to the "hostile class."

The Chinese government fears an invasion of North Korean refugees should the borders to the country open up, and wants things to stay as they are. In South Korea, fewer and fewer seem to think reunification is possible. And in the West, we shake our heads at North Korea. The country is absurd. Human rights activists around the world are sidelined on the North Korea question, because they disrupt the existing "balance of terror" while attempts are made to lure Kim Jong-il to the negotiation table for six-party talks with China, the United States, Japan, South Korea, and Russia. Meanwhile, Kim Jong-il continues to threaten to unleash his atomic monster.

When we look out the window at the landscape rushing past us, everything feels veiled and distant. But would it have helped if we had been here eighty times eight days? Would we have gotten a better understanding? Madame and Shin were here for eight years but were never allowed to engage in conversation with North Koreans who weren't high-ranking.

* * *

AFTER FOUR YEARS in Hollywood, the longing for South Korea grew too strong for Choi Eun-hee and Shin Sang-ok. They tried to return in 1988 but were barred from entering the country; the suspicion around them was too great. The following year they were allowed entry after passing a lie detector test and handing over the gifts they had been given by Kim Jong-il. South Korean officials made a point of taking Shin's Rolex, because it was assumed to be a present from the North Korean leader.

Years of ostracism followed. It was if they had been

infected by their close contact with the enemy. But in spite of everything, Shin was still a legendary director. No one could deny his contribution to South Korean cinema. There was only one way for him to gain acceptance and demonstrate his loyalty: to serve those in power. His 1990 film *Mayumi: Virgin Terrorist* was his ideological penance. *Mayumi* is often cited as his worst film, grotesque in its patriotism and shameless in its propaganda on behalf of the South Korean regime. The film is about the 1987 bombing of a South Korean passenger plane by a North Korean agent — the same story that would later provide the foundation for the mega-hit *Shiri*.

IN 1994 THE couple was finally able to settle permanently in Seoul. The film that Shin made that year had completely different political content. *Disappeared* (*Jeungbal*) is a searing criticism of the political violence during General Park's reign. The kidnapping theme is explored here, but the perpetrator is not Kim Jong-il — it's Park's agents. The story is about the former head of South Korean security, who is about to publish his memoir. But he is kidnapped in Paris and taken to the presidential palace, the Blue House in Seoul. While in captivity, the man has flashbacks of the military coup that brought the dictator to power. Perhaps *Disappeared* was Shin's revenge on General Park, who once tried to end his film career.

IN 1998, *PULGASARI* was shown in a few theatres in Japan. The film was marketed as "forbidden for a decade." Kim Jong-il's idea of reproducing the monster as a plastic toy was finally realized by his arch-enemy. The Tokyo company Marmit made three versions — one red, one black, and one in gold — which could only be bought in cinemas.

During Kim Dae-jung's presidency (1998–2003), there was a period of détente between the countries, until 2008, when Lee Myung-bak, "The Bulldozer," came into power. Certain exchanges were made possible on both sides, not least the reunion of a few families who had been torn apart during the war. In 2000, *Pulgasari* was shown in South Korea for the first time, but it flopped. No one was interested.

That same year, a reporter from the *Financial Times* wrote that Kim Jong-il's image was being reappraised in South Korea after a decade of the Sunshine Policy. What had previously been considered pathetic — his short, chubby body, his blow-dried hair, his platform shoes — had now become a cherished combination: "South Korean schoolchildren are emailing pictures of Mr Kim as a cute cartoon figure and comparing him to the Teletubbies because he 'has a pot belly and is cheerful.'"

Kim Jong-il's first-born son, Kim Jong-nam, so longed for cuteness that in 2001, at the age of thirty, he tried to sneak into Japan using a fake passport in order to visit Disneyland. He was caught at customs. In his fake passport he had given himself a Chinese alias: Pang Xiong, or "Fat Bear."

*   *   *

THE CUSTOMS PROCEDURE at the border is thorough. We share a compartment with Nils and the tattooed baker.

The agents rummage through our luggage. Our camera is inspected. The customs officers look at all the pictures on the digital cameras. Pictures that are not suitable are deleted, but it happens randomly. No one gets to keep pictures of ox-drawn carts—that might imply the country is behind in its development. A few images of certain military men are approved, but our pictures of the colonel who was supposed to show us the wall in the fog are deleted without hesitation. The customs officer points at our analogue SLRs. When he understands that there's nothing to look at, he simply shrugs. We are worried about our video camera, which contains the most interesting material. Our first instinct was to hide it under a blanket, but then we changed our minds. We left it out in the open on the table. No one asked to view its contents.

AFTER A FEW hours of inspection, the train rolls over the bridge to China. The last we see of North Korea is an empty playground with a rusty carousel. Out in the middle of the Yalu River we pass a bridge that suddenly stops short. The bridge was bombed during the Korean War. The Chinese have rebuilt their side, but the North Koreans have shown no interested in rebuilding the bridge to China. We see Chinese people standing on the bridge, binoculars in hand, searching for a glimpse of life on the other side.

*　*　*

IN 2006, SHIN SANG-OK died after battling the hepatitis that he had contracted in the North Korean prison camp.

His life moved in cycles and circles. The same went for Madame. Her private life had been entangled in her acting life, and she came to embody a transitional character, a synthesis between the traditional Korean housewife and a modern, independent woman. She depicted the trials and ambiguities of female life during the post-war period. In *Confessions of a College Student* (1958), she played a lawyer who risks her career defending divorced women. Madame based her character on South Korea's first female lawyer, Lee Tai-young. They became lifelong friends. Madame called her "my second mother."

Madame's portrait of Sonya in *Flower in Hell* contrasts with the widow in *My Mother and Her Guest* (*Sarangbang sonnimgwa eomeoni*)—her favourite among her own films. Whereas the widow is swaddled in her *hanbok* with her hair done in a widow's style, in a tight bun at her neck, Sonya wanders around in high heels and a low-cut dress. The widow can't admit her feelings for her guest. She is a prisoner of all the things that belong to her previous life: photographs, flowers, a piano.

Melodrama draws in audiences by tightening its grip on their emotions. Its aim is to make tears run. Melodrama isn't slick; it's stylized. Douglas Sirk, the great director of Hollywood melodrama, said that the genre "should function for society as Socrates's dialogues and Euripides's melodramas did in ancient Athens." Melodrama plays us as if we were its instrument. We feel it in our bodies. There is also a sacramental element: fear and empathy reach their climax in the sacrifice of one of the characters in the story, a victim whose death cleanses someone else's life.

In melodrama, material things have a strong presence; clothes become transitional objects and markers for the dramatic changes in a character's mind. In his essay titled "Imitation of Life," Rainer Werner Fassbinder, one of the most important directors in New German Cinema, says that Sirk's films are all about what it is possible to say and do in a restricted space. Fassbinder saw what almost no one else saw in Sirk, the German-American director of "weepies" — namely, that the characters in Sirk's films are placed in settings that are shaped by their social situations and have an exactness; you know the limitations of each room. Fassbinder writes:

> Sirk has said: "You can't make films about something; you can only make films with something: with people, with light, with flowers, with mirrors, with blood, in fact with all the crazy things that are worth it."

"We are the victims of history," Madame wrote in her autobiography. She wasn't just talking about herself and Shin, but about all Koreans. "We survived for fifty years, but it feels like we survived for five hundred."

Choi Eun-hee and Shin Sang-ok's lives are written into a political and geographic triangle: Communist dictator, right-wing dictator, and the United States. North, South, and West. Hollywood's influence on Shin Films, which was crushed by General Park and resurrected in North Korea.

Within the same triangle are the atomic bomb and monster movies. The bomb was created in the United States, dropped on Japan, and is now being developed in North Korea. In North Korea, Godzilla became Pulgasari who became Galgameth in Hollywood.

*   *   *

THE TRAIN ROLLS into the station of the Chinese border town of Dandong. After North Korea, the colours here seem shockingly bright. The cars are new — they flash and shine. Billboards clutter the façades. On one sign, an adorable manga policeman encourages drivers to use their seatbelts. *Kawaii* is invading China.

By the time the train leaves Dandong, we are famished. The Bromma boys are sitting in the dining car, gorging on food. Elias has suddenly become their butler. Dressed in an undershirt, he runs around with a wine bottle and serves them. As soon as we take a seat at a table, the waitress snorts at us and shouts: "Go away!" Her teeth point straight out. We try to get help from Bruno, whose size commands respect and who speaks a little Chinese, but Bruno mumbles and the waitress won't listen. We refuse to leave our seats and cast jealous glances at the Bromma boys' teeming table. We are too hungry to give up, and soon the waitress relents and starts procuring rice dishes and Chinese red wine, brusquely setting them on the table.

Darkness falls and we retreat into our compartment. As we drift off, we are woken by a female border control officer who sticks electric thermometers into our ears without a word.

WE ARRIVE IN Beijing the next afternoon. When we step off the train with our baggage, the platform is crowded. Someone shouts that we have to show our tickets in order to leave the station. We have a joint ticket, but we aren't sure which one of us has it. Everyone in the group starts to jog; a few fall behind and it becomes difficult to figure out who's who. At the gate, there's no one asking for a ticket and we are let through without question. Our fellow travellers scatter without us noticing. No goodbyes or exchanging of email addresses. The group melds with the masses. Andrei disappears with his luggage full of unique water samples and other valuable liquids from the hidden world. Bruno and the Swedish fighter pilot are so tall that their heads stick up above the crowd. We watch them move along as if they are suspended from an aerial ropeway, until they are out of sight. The Bromma boys are already hailing a taxi outside the station. The last we see of the group is Ari's grey flat cap gliding away through the crowd.

We are left standing outside the train station. We look around. People are noticeably rounder and taller here than in North Korea; they almost look over-nourished. Their body language is different. A few saunter along, undisciplined. Everyone seems to be moving at their own pace.

By the square outside the station there's a large billboard for a Hello Kitty stage play. Hello Kitty wears a gold rococo gown and her boyfriend, Dear Daniel, is wearing a crown.

They are the king and queen of the universe. And they have come to bring us joy and song.

EPILOGUE

2008–2014

D URING NORTH KOREA'S sixtieth birthday celebrations in September 2008, the international media wondered where Kim Jong-il was hiding. He didn't make an appearance at the enormous military parade on Kim Il-sung Square. It was assumed that he was gravely ill; French and Chinese neurological specialists were flown in to Pyongyang. The press was fed a few images of the leader to quell the speculation around his condition. In one of the pictures, the trees have spring leaves; in another his shadow falls in the wrong direction.

In the late autumn, images were published of Kim Jong-il looking gaunt, one hand stiffly posed and crooked in his pocket—a sign of a stroke. The pictures were unique in their open depiction of the leader's physical demise. At about the same time, songs were being sung in North Korea praising a new General Kim. He was a general whose power "brings joy to the rivers and mountains."

ON APRIL 5, 2009, North Korea launched a three-stage rocket. The North Korean government was irritated by the protests from neighbouring countries. The KCNA quoted a spokesperson from the Ministry of Foreign Affairs who explained that they would promptly reinstate their nuclear weapons program and begin making plutonium again "to handle the increased military threat from enemy powers." On May 25, they conducted another underground atomic test explosion near Kilju.

IN 2009, an enormous sign was held up during a parade in Pyongyang that read: "we cannot live away from his breast" — a sign that from then on was shown whenever "General Kim Jong-il's Song" played on television.

That September, a Taiwanese tourist took a picture of a poster that congratulated the people for having not only the general to tend to their well-being, but also "The Young General Kim Jong-un." The text read that the young general carried the bloodline of Mount Baekdu, which proved that he belonged to the ruling dynasty.

In November, North Korean diplomats were again arrested for smuggling when Swedish customs officers confiscated 230,000 cigarettes. In December the diplomats, a married couple, were sentenced to eight months in prison, which they had to serve because they were not accredited in Sweden.

THROUGHOUT 2010, the South Korean state published full-page ads in the daily newspapers of all the countries that had supported the UN operation during the Korean War—a reminder that war had broken out sixty years ago. It proclaimed thanks to all the countries who fought under the UN flag, as well as those who gave humanitarian aid.

AT THE END of March 2010, a severe crisis between South and North Korea arose after the South Korean battleship ROKS *Cheonan* sank to the bottom of the Yellow Sea near Baengnyeong Island, in South Korean territory at the inter-Korean maritime border. Forty-six seamen died. A team of international experts carrying out the South Korean–led investigation concluded that the battleship had been hit by a torpedo fired from a North Korean midget submarine. North Korea denied any involvement in the sinking of the *Cheonan*. Even Russian experts, the Chinese government, and critics in South Korea questioned the findings of the investigation.

THE NORTH KOREAN national soccer team did not fare well during the World Cup in South Africa later that summer. After a good match against Brazil (North Korea 1–Brazil 2), the mood brightened and it was decided that the next match against Portugal would be broadcast live. It was the first time in history that a soccer game was broadcast live in the country, but it was a disaster and North Korea lost 7–0. During the last part of the match, the North Korean commentator did not say a word. When the team returned to Pyongyang, the coach, Kim Jong-hun, was fired and the whole team was interrogated at a six-hour-long general meeting at the

People's Palace of Culture in Pyongyang. The coach was accused of having betrayed the leader's son Kim Jong-un but he managed to avoid the work camp. He had to start over as a construction worker.

IN MID-SEPTEMBER 2010, the Japanese wrestling star Antonio Inoki, who we had run into in the lobby of the Yanggakdo Hotel, was awarded the North Korean Friendship Medal in Pyongyang. On his way home, he broke the news that the North Korean Workers' Party Conference, which was scheduled for early September, had been postponed. When the conference was finally held on September 28, it was the first time in thirty years that such a meeting had taken place. During the conference, their "superior leadership body" was chosen. Kim Jong-un was named a four-star general, along with Kim Jong-il's sister Kim Kyong-hui. Kim Jong-un was also sworn into the party's Central Committee and was made a member of the Central Military Commission. When January 8 was suddenly declared a national holiday, Western media speculated that the date was the new general's birthday. Then South Korean counterintelligence found a document used in the education of North Korean troops calling Kim Jong-un a "legendary person" and a "genius of geniuses," as well as emphasizing that he had the same holy blood as the Dear Leader.

If all went well, then North Korea would be able to maintain the dynastic continuity that Ernst Kantorowicz spoke of. The rituals of transition had been set in motion by placing the heir as a novice by the ruler's side. In North

Korea, it had never been publicly stated how many children Kim Jong-il had or with which women; these women and children were called by name even less often. Now, with quick side-to-side movements, they had to shine the spotlight on both the current ruler and the heir apparent. The state news agency allowed a photograph to be published in conjunction with the conference in which the son has a somewhat brighter light shining on him.

A massive heroification process lay ahead of them. Stories about and tributes to the ascendant leader had to be presented on all levels and in all places: the daycare centres, the factories, the offices, and the fields. In our age—an age North Korea does belong to—this is a job for the media, which in North Korea still means television, radio, and newspapers. On the radio and in the speakers in people's homes, Kim Jong-un's geniality had to be passed down and sung about every day. Every day the people would have to hear the crackling of that intense, melodramatic voice as it praised his superhuman abilities.

But Kim Jong-un also had to be raised up to the level of a god without overshadowing the still-living leader. It was a difficult task, since the operation had to be coordinated with the ruler's health. Two kings and their two bodies—their physical and political bodies—had to be symbolically bridged. During this transition phase, there is always a risk of rebellion among the people. The transfer of power had probably already happened in de facto terms, but it had to be executed as carefully as possible in public in order to avoid the paralysis of the last succession, or worse—a revolution.

This time there wasn't a presidential post to give to the dead leader. That post is filled for eternity.

IN OCTOBER 2010 the founder of Juche Thought, the defector Hwang Jang-yop, was found dead in his bathtub in his apartment in Seoul. Hwang was eighty-seven years old. He had long been the target of assassination attempts and death threats, but the police insisted he died of natural causes. Soon after his death, police arrested a North Korean agent who had entered South Korea as a defector. This agent had been sent to assassinate Hwang. It was thirteen years since Hwang had defected, but North Korea never forgives. However, an autopsy concluded that the Juche philosopher died of a heart attack, and so the North Koreans were robbed of their revenge.

ON NOVEMBER 21, the *New York Times* reported that the North Korean authorities had presented a new ultra-modern uranium enrichment facility to the American nuclear scientist Siegfried S. Hecker. Hecker was stunned to silence when faced with the hundreds of centrifuges and the control rooms, and he later confirmed that the plant could easily be adapted to produce highly enriched uranium, which is used in the manufacturing of nuclear weapons.

Two days later, a minor war broke out between North and South Korea. Pyongyang had warned the South against continuing their military exercises in the waters around the South Korean island Yeonpyeong. When the South Korean government refused, the North Korean military fired dozens of artillery shells at the island. Houses burned and the population fled in fishing boats. South Korea responded with gunfire and bombs, and President Lee Myung-bak threatened "severe retribution." North Korea in turn threatened further attacks if the neighbouring country trespassed on the disputed sea boundaries "by even 0.001 millimetres."

ON DECEMBER 19, 2011, Kim Jong-il's death was announced on KCTV. The message was delivered by Ri Chun-hee, North Korea's most famous news anchor. Ri had also relayed the news of Kim Il-sung's death seventeen years earlier. She cried throughout the broadcast, just as she had then.

Reports from the state news bureau told of strange natural phenomena. Bears woke from their winter sleep and could be seen wandering sorrowfully among wolves. Magpies and cranes circled around statues of Kim Il-sung. In the early morning on the very day of his death, December 17, the ice on Mount Baekdu's crater lake unleashed a roaring sound, whereupon a furious snowstorm raged over the landscape. Nature's convulsions of sorrow broke at dawn: all fell still, and the light of a blood-red sun stained the peaks of the revolutionary mountain. Great masses of people gathered at the monuments in Pyongyang and howled in sorrow. People fell to their knees and pounded their fists on the stone steps.

On December 28 the hearse was driven through Pyongyang's snow-covered streets, and every one of the city's residents seemed to be out in the cold to say goodbye to the Dear Leader.

The following day, Kim Jong-un was proclaimed the Great Successor.

IN APRIL 2012, Kim Jong-un was named First Secretary of the Workers' Party of Korea. At the same time, the position of General Secretary became forever occupied, as Kim Jong-il, like his father, was honoured with an eternal title. Kim Jong-un delivered his first speech, which was a clear sign of his new role as leader. In contrast to his father, he was outgoing and spoke directly to the people.

The year 2012 also marked the centenary of Kim Il-sung's birth. In honour of the Day of the Sun celebrations, the state scheduled a long-range missile test, but it failed. According to North Korea, the aim of the launch was to shoot down an orbiting satellite. The United States and Japan said it was really a poorly veiled test that, yet again, threatened the security of the region. In December, North Korea's luck turned around and it managed to launch a rocket into orbit, causing a great swell of national pride. During the autumn, the official North Korean rhetoric was full of bombastic threats toward the rest of the world. It was asserted that their missiles would have no problem reaching the continental United States.

Twenty-five years after construction began, the country met their goal of finishing the Ryugyong Hotel ("the Death Star") in time for the centennial. Well, the immense glass façade was finished, and the hotel achieved its full expression as a structure that looked like it was straight out of a science fiction movie. Inside, however, it was still empty.

Pictures were published showing the bare concrete of the garage-like lobby.

ON FEBRUARY 12, 2013, the country carried out its third nuclear weapons test, again at Punggye-ri Nuclear Test Site in Kilju. The United Nations Security Council implemented new sanctions as punishment, and the United States and South Korea ramped up their military training exercises. Pyongyang's senior military leaders called a meeting after two U.S. B-2 bombers, flying out of bases in Missouri, carried out simulated bombing raids on North Korean targets on an island off the coast of South Korea. The North Korean government considered this act a declaration of war. It was announced that operations would be resumed at the nuclear energy facility in Yongbyon, which had been closed since 2007, and short-range ballistic missiles tests would begin.

The KCNA published pictures that smacked of the Cold War. Kim Jong-un appeared to be at a command centre, strategizing at a glossy desk, with three large, identical telephones at his side. He seemed to be plotting military action against the United States. In the background of one of the images is a map marked with targets for a rocket attack bearing the text U.S. MAINLAND STRIKE PLAN. The generals that surround the leader are holding notepads, awaiting orders. Over 100,000 soldiers, fists clenched, gathered on Kim Il-sung Square in Pyongyang to proclaim their hatred of the United States.

DURING THE SECOND half of 2013, North Korea's aggressive line asserting that it was in a state of war abruptly shifted.

The industrial zone in Kaesong, which had been closed off to South Koreans since April, was reopened. The KCNA claimed that Buddhists had gathered in all of the temples in North Korea to pray for reunification.

In December, a bloody purge of the upper echelons of the North Korean government began. Of the seven men who had escorted Kim Jong-il's hearse on foot, five disappeared within a short amount of time. Some lost their positions; others were executed. One of those executed—Jang Song-thaek—was considered the second-most powerful person in the country, after the leader. Furthermore, he had blood ties to the ruling clan—he was married to Kim Jong-un's aunt Kim Kyong-hui. Jang was accused of being a corrupt, drug-addled Casanova and a traitor who had tried to build his own platform of power within the party. The long list of accusations is fascinating. He was said to have amassed wealth by instructing his underlings to sell "coal and other precious underground resources." He was accused of gambling at a casino, distributing pornography, and opposing the construction of new monuments. Not least, he is said to have tried to stop the installation of a mosaic depicting Kim Il-sung and Kim Jong-il, and to have ordered that Kim Jong-un's signature be chiselled in granite in the wrong place on an official building, so that it was cast in shadow.

Kim Chol, vice-minister of the North Korean Army, was another unlucky dignitary. In his case, there were no official accusations, only speculation. The South Korean media suggested that the reason Kim Chol was executed was because he had not displayed a sufficient amount of grief after the death of Kim Jong-il. He'd been caught carousing during the "one hundred days of mourning" and was judged harshly by Kim Jong-un. According to the *Chosun Ilbo* he was executed via launched explosive on a mortar range. On the orders of the leader, they were to leave "no trace of him behind, down to his hair."

That same year, there were new reports of the sea monster in Heaven Lake. A functionary on the Chinese side, who measured the water temperature and took gas samples with a colleague, spied a creature in the water. He took a number of blurry photographs that were supposed to show a deer-like head jutting through the water's surface.

AT THE START of 2014, the icy relations between North and South Korea began to thaw. On February 12, representatives from both governments met in the demilitarized zone. During the meeting, imminent reunification of a number of families that had been separated since the Korean War was discussed. At the same time, the United Nations published a new report about conditions in North Korea. The 372-page document was seen as the most exhaustive and reliable account of the violence that had been carried out during the Kim clan's rule. It is merciless in its descriptions of human rights violations in the country: a total lack of freedom of speech, slavery, execution because of "disloyalty to the State," concentration camps where torture, rape, and forced abortions are carried out. The report also condemns North Korea's most unique contribution to the dark list of crimes against humanity: the systematic kidnapping of carefully selected foreign nationals.

NOTE ON SOURCES AND THANKS

Korean names have been written according to Korean convention with the surname first. Japanese names have been written in Western fashion with the given name followed by the surname.

CERTAIN SOURCES HAVE been especially important for our work on *All Monsters Must Die*.

Bradley K. Martin's *Under the Loving Care of the Fatherly Leader: North Korea and the Kim Dynasty*, Bertil Lintner's *Great Leader, Dear Leader: Demystifying North Korea under the Kim Clan*, and Selig S. Harrison's *Korean Endgame: A Strategy for Reunification and U.S. Disengagement* were our main sources on North Korean history, as well as facts and theories about the ruling clan.

Through his studies of internal communication in North Korea (literature, propaganda, communiques, news media, and documents), B. R. Myers has formulated a series of original theories about the North Korean self-perception in *The Cleanest Race: How North Koreans See Themselves and Why It Matters*. His book has helped us understand what lies behind the country's isolation policy, nationalism, and extreme racial ideology. Some of Myers's ideas about the formation of the image of Kim Il-sung as a ruling figure touch on anthropologist Roy Richard Grinker's thoughts in *Korea and Its Futures: Unification and the Unfinished War*.

Regarding information about North Korea's economic situation, the country's media landscape, and developments after the catastrophic famine, we are deeply indebted to Ralph Hassig and Oh Kongdan's *The Hidden People of North Korea: Everyday Life in the Hermit Kingdom*. The book is based on 200 interviews they conducted with North Korean defectors at the end of the 1990s. It should be said that the authors cite lower numbers (between 600,000 and 1 million) in their estimation of the number of people who died during the famine than what is normally cited (around 2 million). The authors harbour strong hope for the relaxation of economic systems of control, cross-border trade with China, and concessions in the planned economy for future democratic changes in the country — phenomena that Myers brushes off as naive hopes.

Our experience of North Korea as a nation where performances, films, and choreography permeate society often coincides with Professor Kim Suk-young's ideas around performance studies. Her lectures and essays have been collected in *Illusive Utopia: Theater, Film, and Everyday Performance in North Korea*—possibly the only thorough study of the North Korean social system from a culture-theory perspective.

When it comes to interludes on Japanese monster movies, David Kalat's *A Critical History and Filmography of Toho's Godzilla Series* and William Tsutsui's *Godzilla on My Mind* have been invaluable. Both books are innovative in their theories about Godzilla as a cultural metaphor and stem from a true *kaiju*-fan's body of knowledge. For the technical aspects behind Japanese monster movies and the historical context, August Ragone's book about special effects artist Eiji Tsuburaya is an indispensable reference—*Eiji Tsuburaya: Master of Monsters* explores all the films that Tsuburaya worked on, how he developed his techniques, and his importance in Japanese cinema as a whole.

For the parts of the book that address cuteness (*kawaii*) and its place in Japanese contemporary culture, the essays of Carl Cassegård and Sianne Ngai have been sources of inspiration, especially their political reading of "cute" in Japanese culture (Cassegård) and as an aesthetic category in general (Ngai).

The main source for Choi Eun-hee and Shin Sang-ok's story is our own five-hour-long conversation with Madame Choi in Seoul on July 18, 2007. We've taken some details from her autobiography *Gobaek*, but also from Michael Breen's book *Kim Jong-Il: North Korea's Dear Leader*. We want to extend a large thanks to Choi Eun-hee for so generously sharing her life story. A special thanks to Kwak Hyun-jin for the translation of Choi Eun-hee's autobiography, for help with Korean terminology, and for the insight into Korean culture.

Sten Bergman's travel stories of occupied Korea are deeply coloured by the colonial power relationships at that time. The Japanese ruling perspective is even more dominant in the English translation (*In Korean Wilds and Villages*): all the Korean names are written in Japanese, and the Koreans in general are presented as relatively primitive and helpless — in need of a protective power.

For knowledge about the Swedish North and South Korea debate and reflections on Korean events in Sweden, the Sigtuna Foundation Library's archive of press cuttings has been a gold mine.

An equally important archive has been the Korean Film Archive in Seoul, where we had the opportunity to view many of Choi Eun-hee and Shin Sang-ok's productions. For the archival work in Seoul, the knowledge and translations of the artist Jo Ha-young and the theatre researcher Kim Tae-hyung have been essential.

We also want to thank Choi Sun-kyoung, Huh Sookyoung, Mårten Frankby, Will Oldham, Svante Weyler, Dilsa Demirbag-Sten, Kim Sunjung/SAMUSO, Seoul (Platform -09), RAS-I, the Headlands Center for the Arts in San Francisco, and the Arts Initiative Tokyo, as well as our fellow travellers in North Korea.

Our research trips have been made possible by means from the Swedish Authors' Fund, the Längmanska Cultural

Foundation, Helge Ax:son Johnson Foundation, and Konstfack, as well as the Harald and Louise Ekman Research
Foundation. Parts of our research overlap with *You Told
Me: Work Stories and Video Essays*—a dissertation in artistic
research by Magnus Bärtås at the Valand Academy/Univer-
sity of Gothenburg.

BIBLIOGRAPHY

BOOKS

Bergman, Sten. *I morgonstillhetens land* [In Korean Wilds and Villages]. Albert Bonniers Förlag, 1952.

———. *In Korean Wilds and Villages.* Travel Book Club, 1938.

Bergström, Villy, and Benjamin Katzeff Silberstein. *Bilder från Nordkorea* [Pictures from North Korea]. Bokförlaget Atlas, 2010.

——— and Kurt Wickman. *Bilder från Nordkorea* [Pictures from North Korea]. Tidens Förlag, 1972.

Breen, Michael. *Kim Jong-Il: North Korea's Dear Leader.* John Wiley & Sons, 2004.

Carlsson, Cajsa, and Ulf-Göran Widqvist. *Sydkorea: undrets baksida* [South Korea: The Other Side of Wonder]. Språkmakar'n, 1988.

Chatwin, Bruce. *What Am I Doing Here?* Brombergs Bokförlag, 2002.

Chinoy, Mike. *Meltdown: The Inside Story of the North Korean Nuclear Crisis*. St. Martin's Griffin, 2008.

Choi, Eun-hee. *Gobaek*. Random House Korea, 2007.

Chung, Steven. *Split Screen Korea: Shin Sang-ok and Postwar Cinema*. University of Minnesota Press, 2014.

Cornell, Erik. *Nordkorea: sändebud till paradiset* [North Korea under Communism: Report of an Envoy to Paradise]. Studentlitteratur, 1999.

Delisle, Guy. *Pyongyang: A Journey in North Korea*. Drawn & Quarterly, 2005.

Demick, Barbara. *Nothing to Envy: Ordinary Lives in North Korea*. Spiegel & Grau, 2009.

Ehnmark, Anders. *Arvskifte: 5 politiska memoarer* [Estate Distribution: 5 Political Memoirs]. Norstedts, 1989.

Fitzgerald, Frances. *Way Out There in the Blue: Reagan, Star Wars and the End of the Cold War*. Simon & Schuster, 2000.

Frederking, Brian. *The United States and the Security Council: Collective Security Since the Cold War*. Routledge, 2007.

Grinker, Roy Richard. *Korea and Its Futures: Unification and the Unfinished War*. Macmillan, 2000.

Harrison, Selig S. *Korean Endgame: A Strategy for Reunification and U.S. Disengagement*. Princeton University Press, 2002.

Hassig, Ralph, and Kongdan Oh. *The Hidden People of North Korea: Everyday Life in the Hermit Kingdom*. Rowman & Littlefield, 2009.

Hauser, Arnold. *The Social History of Art*. Vols. I–IV. Routledge, 1999.

Hyok, Kang. *This is Paradise!: My North Korean Childhood*. Abacus, 2009.

Hyun, Peter. *Darkness at Dawn: A North Korean Diary*. Hanjin Publishing Company, 1981.

Kalat, David. *A Critical History and Filmography of Toho's Godzilla Series*. McFarland & Company, 2007.

Kang, Chol-hwan, and Pierre Rigoulot. *The Aquariums of Pyongyang: Ten Years in a North Korean Gulag*. Basic Books, 2001.

Kantorowicz, Ernst H. *The King's Two Bodies: A Study in Mediaeval Political Theology*. Princeton University Press, 1957.

Kim, Il-sung. *On Juche in Our Revolution*. Bo Cavefors Bokförlag, 1978.

Kim, Jong-il. *On the Art of the Cinema*. University Press of the Pacific, 2001.

Kim, Suk-young. *Illusive Utopia: Theater, Film, and Everyday Performance in North Korea*. University of Michigan Press, 2010.

Lee, Hyangjin. *Contemporary Korean Cinema: Identity, Culture and Politics*. Manchester University Press, 2000.

Lintner, Bertil. *Great Leader, Dear Leader: Demystifying North Korea under the Kim Clan*. Silkworm Books, 2005.

Lönn, Jan. *Nordkorea: mot välfärd under krigshot* [North Korea: Towards Social Welfare under the Threat of War]. Bokförlaget Pan/Norstedts, 1972.

Lowe, Peter. *The Origins of The Korean War*. Longman, 1997.

Marrero, Robert. *Godzilla: King of the Movie Monsters*. Fantasma Books, 1996.

Martin, Bradley K. *Under the Loving Care of the Fatherly Leader: North Korea and the Kim Dynasty.* Thomas Dunne Books, 2004.

McHugh, Kathleen, and Nancy Abelmann, eds. *South Korean Golden Age Melodrama: Gender, Genre, and National Cinema.* Wayne State University Press, 2005.

Min, Eungjin, Jinsook Joo, and Han Ju Kwak. *Korean Film: History, Resistance, and Democratic Imagination.* Praeger Publishers, 2003.

Murakami, Takashi, ed. *Little Boy: The Arts of Japan's Exploding Subculture.* Japan Society Gallery/Yale University Press, 2005.

Myers, B. R. *The Cleanest Race: How North Koreans See Themselves and Why It Matters.* Melville House, 2009.

Nielsen, Aage Krarup. *Från Korea till Bali* [From Korea to Bali]. Albert Bonniers Förlag, 1952.

Nye Jr., Joseph S. *Soft Power: The Means to Success in World Politics.* PublicAffairs, 2004.

Oberdorfer, Don. *The Two Koreas: A Contemporary History.* Basic Books, 2001.

Racine, Jean. *The Complete Plays of Jean Racine.* Vol. 2, *Bajazet.* Translated by Geoffrey Alan Argent. Penn State University Press, 2010.

Ragone, August. *Eiji Tsuburaya: Master of Monsters: Defending the Earth with Ultraman, Godzilla, and Friends in the Golden Age of Japanese Science Fiction Film.* Chronicle Books, 2007.

Salzinger, Caroline. *Hälsningar från ondskans axelmakter: vardag och vansinne i världens mest stängda länder* [Greetings from Evil's Axis Powers: The Everyday and Insanity in the World's Most Closed-off Countries]. Bokförlaget DN, 2007.

Satsuma, Kenpachiro. *Ore ha haiyu da*. Wides Shuppan, 2004.

Schönherr, Johannes. *North Korean Cinema: History*. McFarland & Company, 2012.

Sereny, Gitta. *Albert Speer och sanningen*. Bonnier Alba, 1997.

Shin, Sang-ok, and Eun-hee Choi. *Uriui talchulun kkutnaji anatta*. Wolgan Joseeonsa, 2001.

Tsutsui, William. *Godzilla on My Mind: Fifty Years of the King of Monsters*. Palgrave Macmillan, 2004.

ESSAYS, ARTICLES, ONLINE PUBLICATIONS, WEBSITES, AND DOCUMENTARIES

Ahn, Yonson. "China and the Two Koreas Clash Over Mount Paekdu/Changbai: Memory Wars Threaten Regional Accommodation." *The Asia-Pacific Journal: Japan Focus*, July 27, 2007.

"Alleged Communists Massacred under the Eyes of American Soldiers." *The Observers*, June 13, 2008.

Anrup, Roland. "Det socialistiska Korea" [The Socialist Korea]. *Sydsvenska Dagbladet*, February 13, 1972.

Azuma, Hirko. "Superflat Japanese Postmodernity." *The Daily Impressionist*, November 4, 2010.

Bellini, Andrea, and Chiara Leoni. "Takashi Murakami: A Japanese Character." *Flash Art* 39 (2006).

Bennett, Bruce. "A Life in the Red." *New York Sun*, August 10, 2007.

Bergström, Villy. "Hur bedöms Nordkorea?" [How Do We Evaluate North Korea?]. *Aftonbladet*, March 12, 1973.

Booker, Paula. "Red Stars." *New Zealand Listener*, October 13–19, 2007.

Braw, Monica. "Nordkoreas ledare mördad" [North Korea's Leader Killed]. *Svenska Dagbladet*, November 18, 1986.

Bärtås, Magnus, and Fredrik Ekman. "Det mentala tonårsrummet" [The Teenage Room of the Mind]. *Tidskriften Index* 2 (1996).

———. "All Monsters Must Die: Godzilla's Children Go to North Korea." *Cabinet Magazine* 35 (2009).

Cassegård, Carl. "Från gullighetskult till nationalism" [From the Cult of Cute to Nationalism]. *Glänta* 3 (2006).

Cheung, Star. "Explanation of Mysterious 'Tianchi Monster.'" china.org.cn, November 15, 2007.

Choe, Sang-hun. "North Korean Leader Stresses Need for Strong Military." *New York Times*, April 15, 2002.

Choe, Sang-hun. "South Koreans Struggle with Race." *New York Times*, November 11, 2009.

Croddy, Eric. "Vinalon, the DPRK, and Chemical Weapons Precursors." *NTI*, February 2003.

Crossing the Line. Documentary (2007), directed by Daniel Gordon. Broadcast on SVT2, April 28, 2008.

Dahlin, Leif. "Nordkoreas urusla finanser smuggelorsak" [North Korea's Ailing Finances Cause for Smuggling]. *Dagens Nyheter*, October 20, 1976.

Demetriou, Danielle. "Kim Jong-il: A Typical North Korean State Funeral." *Daily Telegraph*, December 28, 2011.

Demick, Barbara. "Rich Taste in a Poor Country." *Los Angeles Times*, June 26, 2006.

Diffrient, David Scott. "Han'guk Heroism: Cinematic Spectacle and the Postwar Cultural Politics of *Red Muffler*," in *South Korean Golden Age Melodrama: Gender, Genre, and National Cinema*, edited by Kathleen McHugh and Nancy Abelmann. Wayne State University Press, 2005.

DiPietro, Monty. "Takashi Murakami at Parco Gallery." September 14, 2009. http://www.assemblylanguage.com/reviews/Murakami.html.

Ehnmark, Anders. "Folkarmén och USA:s soldater" [The People's Army and American Soldiers]. *Expressen*, September 11, 1971.

———. "Varför blev det krig i Korea?" [Why the Korean War?]. *Expressen*, October 12, 1971.

Engblom, Johan. "Korea kan bara förstås genom schamanismen" [Korea Can Only Be Understood through Shamanism]. *Svenska Dagbladet*, March 30, 2005.

Eriksson, Jörgen I. "Kimkultens roll" [The Role of the Kim Cult]. *Dagens Nyheter*, September 20, 1971.

Fassbinder, Rainer Werner. "Imitation av liv" [Imitation of Life], in *Play It Again, Sam: tjugo texter om film och TV* [Play It Again Sam: Twenty Texts on Film and TV]. Filmhäftets förlag, 1984.

Feffer, John. "Screening North Korea." Foreign Policy in Focus, June 12, 2007. http://www.fpif.org/articles/screening_north_korea.

———. "North Korea's Dear Film Buff." *Asia Times*, June 15, 2007.

Filosofisk Tidskrift 3 (1981) [unsigned source].

Gallagher, Tag. "White Melodrama: Douglas Sirk." *Senses of Cinema* 36 (2005).

Gateward, Frances. "Youth in Crisis: National and Cultural Identity in New South Korean Cinema," in *Multiple Modernities, Cinemas and Popular Media in Transcultural East Asia*, edited by Jenny Kwok Wah Lau. Temple University Press, 2003.

Gills, Barry K. "The Coup That Never Happened: The Anatomy of the 'Death' of Kim Il Sung." *Bulletin of Concerned Asian Scholars* 19 (1987).

Gombeaud, Adrien. "A Conversation with Shin San-ok." Koreanfilm.org, December 23, 2000. http://koreanfilm.org/shinsangokk.html.

Gorenfeld, John. "The Producer From Hell." *Guardian*, April 4, 2003.

————. "Hail to the Moon King." Salon.com, June 21, 2004. http://dir.salon.com/news/feature/2004/06/21/moon/index.html.

————. "Dear Leader's Paper Moon." *American Prospect*, June 19, 2005.

Gourevitch, Philip. "The Madness of Kim Jong Il." *Observer Magazine*, February 11, 2003.

Grassmuck, Volker. "'I'm Alone, But Not Lonely.' Japanese Otaku-kids Colonize the Realm of Information and Media: A Tale of Sex and Crime from a Faraway Place." 1990. http://waste.informatik.hu-berlin.de/grassmuck/texts/otaku.e.html.

Gunnarsson, Bo. "9-årige Lee blev nationalmartyr." [9-Year-Old Lee Became National Martyr]. *Dagens Nyheter*, July 24, 1977.

Hagberg, Eva. "The Worst Building in the History of Mankind." *Esquire*, January 28, 2008.

Han, Aaron, and Joon Magnan Park. "Remember Me, Remember Us, Remember Korea: Hallyu, Flashbacks and the Transformations of South Korea into a Unforgettable Nation." *Joint U.S.–Korea Academic Studies* (2008).

Hanley, Charles J., and Jae-soon Chang. "The Truth about Mass Killings in Korea Revealed." *Daily Herald*, June 18, 2008.

Hanaoki, Mimi. "Wrestler, Statesman, Hostage Negotiator, Legend: The Life of Antonio Inoki." *Grantland*, July 22, 2014. http://grantland.com/features/antonio-inoki-japan-politics-pro-wrestling-ric-flair-saddam-hussein-iraq-north-korea-kim-jong-un-hostages/.

Hasegawa, Yumi Wijers. "Princess of Pure Mystery." *Japan Times*, February 4, 2007.

Hauser, Arnold. "Konstnärsroll och samhälle" [The Role of the Artist and Society]. *Konstrevyn* 5–6 (1969).

Hernbäck, Eva. "Nordkorea: Personkult, disciplin" [North Korea: Cult of Personality, Discipline]. *Dagens Nyheter*, September 8, 1971.

———. "Kult kring Kim som vet allt" [The Cult of Kim Who Knows Everything]. *Dagens Nyheter*, September 13, 1971.

———. "'Inga främmande idéer': Ideologin i Nordkorea genomsyrar samhället" ['No Foreign Ideas': The Ideology in North Korea Permeates Society]. *Dagens Nyheter*, September 17, 1971.

———. "Gratis daghem och frivillig militärtjänst" [Free Daycare and Voluntary Military Service]. *Dagens Nyheter*, October 4, 1971.

"How to Read a Closed Book: The Propaganda Signs of North Korea, from Google Earth." http://freekorea.us/

Howard, Young. "The Hidden Gulag." *San Diego Union Tribune*, June 15, 2005.

Isaksson, David. "Schack och religion i Kalmuckien" [Chess and Religion in Kalmykia]. *Norrköpings Tidningar*, February 29, 2008.

Ito, Mizuko. "Hello Kitty Has No Mouth." *Chanpon*. http://www.chanpon.org/archive/2005/12/01/05h28m39s.

Jaggi, Maya. "A Life in Writing: Mourid Barghouti." *Guardian*, December 13, 2008.

Joyce, Andrew. "Antonio Inoki: Wrestling North Korea to Diplomacy?" *Wall Street Journal*, "Japan Real Time," October 12, 2010.

Jung, Sung-ki. "Western Mixed Race Men Can Join Military." *Korean Times*, January 14, 2008.

Kim, Jong-il. "Socialism is a Science." http://www.uk-songun.com.

Kim, Mi-young, and Jon Herskovitz. "North Korea Says Plutonium Extraction Has Started." Reuters, April 25, 2009.

Kim, Myun-jong. "Film Guru Shin Sang-ok Tells of Kim Jong-il." *Seoul Times*, 2005.

Kim, Suk-young. "'Guests' of the Dear Leader: Shin Sang-ok, Choi Eun-hee, and North Korea's Cultural Crisis." *Joint U.S.– Korea Academic Studies* (2008).

Kim, Yong-lun. "City of Revolution with no Warmth of Human." *Daily nk*, October 28, 2005.

Kim, Young-soon. Testimony before the United States Congress, House Committee on Foreign Affairs on Africa, Global Health and Human Rights, on September 20, 2011. http://chrissmith.house.gov/uploadedfiles/testimony_of_kim_young_soon.pdf.

Kims vänner [Friends of Kim]. Documentary (2006), directed by Raphael Wilking and Hans van Dijk. Broadcast on svt2, May 20, 2007.

Kristof, Nicholas. "North Korea's Secret." *New York Times*, January 14, 2003.

Lamm, Lovisa. "Man badar inte naken i Pyongyang" [You Don't Swim Naked in Pyongyang]. Radio broadcast on Sveriges Radio P1, February 14, 2009.

Lankov, Andrej. "Pyongyang and Its People (Notes of a Soviet Student)," from *Severnaia Koreia: vchera i segodnia*. Vostochnaia literatura, 1995.

————. "Body Snatching, North Korean Style." *Asia Times*, February 26, 2005.

Lans, Karl. "Kim Jong Il beslagtar japanska bilar" [Kim Jong Il Confiscates Japanese Cars]. *Dagens Industri*, February 19, 2007.

Larsson, Mats. "Diktatorn firar med basket och terror" [Dictator Celebrates With Basketball and Terror]. *Expressen*, July 1, 2014.

————. "Yngste sonen tar över – men ett familjedrama lurar i kulisserna" [Youngest Son Takes Over, but a Family Drama Is waiting in the Rafters]. *Expressen*, October 29, 2010.

Lee, Jae-bong. "U.S. Deployment of Nuclear Weapons in 1950s South Korea and North Korea's Nuclear Development: Toward Denuclearization of the Korean Peninsula." *The Asia-Pacific Journal: Japan Focus*, http://www.japanfocus.org/-Lee-Jae_Bong/3053.

Lönn, Jan. "Varför erkänns inte Nordkorea?" [Why Isn't North Korea Accepted?]. *Arbetet*, March 10, 1971.

————. "Nordkorea: Jan Lönn om Villy Bergström" [North Korea: Jan Lönn on Villy Bergström]. *Aftonbladet*, March 27, 1973.

Maass, Peter. "The Last Emperor." *New York Times*, October 19, 2003.

Malkin, Bonnie. "North and South Korea Hold High-Level Meeting." *Daily Telegraph*, February 12, 2014.

McGray, Douglas. "Japan's Gross National Cool." http://www.douglasmcgray.com/grossnationalcool.pdf.

Meyer, Richard E. "Pueblo's Bittersweet Tribute." *Los Angeles Times*, May 5, 1990.

Mihm, Stephen. "No Ordinary Counterfeit." *New York Times*, July 23, 2006.

Myers, B. R. "North Korea: Nothing Has Changed." *The Atlantic*, November 2008.

Namgung, Min. "$800000 Spent Preserving Kim Il Sung's Body." *The Daily NK*, April 16, 2008.

Neff, Robert. "Korean Tigers Back from the Brink of Extinction, Except in South Korea." *The Marmot's Hole*, February 6, 2009. http://www.rjkoehler.com/2009/02/06/korean-tigers-back-from-the-brink-of- extinction-except-in-south-korea/

Ngai, Sianne. "The Cuteness of the Avant-Garde." *Critical Inquiry* (2005).

"N. Korea's Kim Died in 2003; Replaced by a Lookalike Says Waseda Professor." *Japan Today*, August 26, 2008.

Norimitsu, Onishi. "In a Country That Craved Respect, Stem Cell Scientist Rode a Wave of Korean Pride." *New York Times*, February 22, 2006.

"North Korea is a Major Player in Animation Industry." Spero News, February 12, 2007. http://www.speroforum.com/site/article.asp?id=7876.

O'Carroll, Chad. "North Korea Executes 'Traitor' Jang Song Thaek." nk.news.org, December 12, 2013. http://www.nknews.org/2013/12/north-korea-executes-jang-song-thaek-for-factionalism/.

Parry, Robert, "Rev. Moon, the Bushes & Donald Rumsfeld." *Consortium News,* January 3, 2001. http://www.consortiumnews.com/2001/010301a.html.

von Platen, Gustaf. "Olympiskt guld i konsten att jobba" [Olympic Gold in the Art of Working]. *Svenska Dagbladet,* March 18, 1979.

————. "Det sydkoreanska undret: varken demokrati eller diktatur" [The South Korean Wonder: Neither Democracy nor Dictatorship]. *Svenska Dagbladet,* April 8, 1979.

Prynne, Miranda. "U.S. Researchers Are Using the Internet to Reveal What Life Is Really Like Behind the Closed Borders of the World's Last Stalinist Dictatorship." *Independent,* May 15, 2009.

————. "North Korea Uncovered: Palaces, Labour Camps and Mass Graves." *Independent,* June 21, 2009.

http://www.pyongyang-metro.com

http://www.pyongyangtrafficgirls.com

"Report of the Detailed Findings of the Commission of the Inquiry on Human Rights in the Democratic People's Republic of Korea." Human Rights Council, February 7, 2014.

Rhee, Jooyeon. "Arirang, and the Making of a National Narrative in South and North Korea." *Journal of Japanese and Korean Cinema* 1.1 (2009).

Rose, David. "North Korea's Dollar Store." *Vanity Fair*, August 5, 2010.

http://ryugyong.org [Site for the Ryugyong Hotel; users can create their own room in the still-unfinished building].

Salomon, Andrew. "Child Born in a Secret Labour Camp Tells of Torture and Beatings." *The Times*, October 30, 2007.

Sawaragi, Noi. "Dangerously Cute: Noi Sawaragi and Fumio Nanjo Discuss Contemporary Japanese Culture." *Flash Art* 163 (March–April 1992).

Schönherr, Johannes. "Films for the Great Leader? Mysterious Film Deals by North Korean Diplomatic Mission in Berlin." *Film International* 16 (2005).

————. "Godzilla Goes to North Korea: An Interview with Kenpachiro Satsuma," in *Film Out of Bounds: Essays and Interviews on Non-Mainstream Cinema Worldwide*, edited by Matthew Edwards. McFarland & Company, 2007.

Seo, Young-il. "The Epic from the North." SOP (Student Operated Press), June 18, 2006. http://thesop.org/story/entertainment/2006/07/28/the-epic-from-the-north.php.

Shanker, Tom. "U.S. Run Practice Sortie in South Korea." *New York Times*, March 28, 2013.

"Sighting of Strange Creature Reported in China's Highest Alpine Lake." *Epoch Times*, August 7, 2013. http://www.theepochtimes.com/n3/235155-strange-creature-sighted-in-china/.

Sjögren, Alf. "Staffanstorpsbor återvänder till Korea efter 58 år" [Residents from Staffanstorp Return to Korea After 58 Years]. *Sydsvenska Dagbladet*, September 3, 2008.

Swartz, Richard. "Diktatorn ser till att aldrig bli ansvarig" [The Dictator Makes Sure He'll Never Be Held Responsible]. *Svenska Dagbladet*, November 28, 2006.

"Tianchi Lake Monster Video." http://www.cryptomundo.com/cryptozoo-news/tianchi6video/.

Toor, Amar. "North Korea Has Committed Crimes against Humanity: UN Report." *The Verge*, February 17, 2014. http://www.theverge.com/2014/2/17/5418586/north-korea-has-committed-crimes-against-humanity-un-report.

Tralau, John. "En skenbart motsägelsefull Leviathan" [A Seemingly Contradictory Leviathan]. *Svenska Dagbladet*, May 10, 2004.

"Two Koreas' Top Brass Resort to Racist Mudslinging." *Chosun Ilbo*, May 17, 2006.

Wagner, Wieland. "Hyundai's Holiday Gulag." *Spiegel* Online, March 13, 2006.

Waldenström, Louise, "Juche: diktatur maskerad som extrem frihet" [Juche: A Dictatorship Masked with Extreme Freedom]. *Svenska Dagbladet*, December 27, 2005.

Watts, Jonathan. "Welcome to the Strangest Show on Earth." *Guardian*, October 10, 2005.

Williamson, Lucy. "North Korea Defies Warnings in Rocket Launch Success." BBC News Asia, December 12, 2012. http://www.bbc.co.uk/news/world-asia-20690338.

Wolodarski, Peter. "Bildning för en riksbankschef" [An Education for the Head of the Riksbank]. *Dagens Nyheter,* December 24, 2005.

"Wrestler an Unlikely Icon for North Korea." *Taipei Times,* July 21, 2003.

INDEX

Abshier, Larry, 157, 158
Air Koryo, 10–11, 28, 94–95
Albright, Madeleine, 87
Ali, Muhammad, 134
animation industry, 19–20
Anyang Studios, 175–76
"Arirang" (folk song), 98
Arirang (silent film), 98–99
Arirang Festival (Mass Games),
   98–102
Atlas Copco, 25, 169
atomic bomb. *See* nuclear bombing,
   by U.S., *and entries following*

Baekdu, Mount, 12, 71–77, 88, 100,
   124, 234, 239; Kim Il-sung birthday
   tribute on, 72–73; Kim Jong-il's
   birthplace on, 73, 80, 88. *See also*
   Heaven Lake
Bavaria Film Studios (Munich), 146
Berdymuchamedov, Gurbanguly, 107
Bergman, Ingrid, 172
Bergman, Sten, 74; *In Korean Wilds
   and Villages*, 74–75
Bergqvist, Lars, 58
Bergström, Villy, 77–80; and *Pictures
   from North Korea*, 78
Beria, Lavrentiy, 82

blood purity, as important to South
   Korea, 65–66
blood ties in North Korea: and class
   system, 117; of Kim Jong-un, 234,
   236; and punishment of family
   members, 42–43, 45, 46, 65, 242; of
   Rikidōzan, 133
Boeri, Stefano, 27
Burchett, Wilfred, 79–80
Bureau 39 (Workers' Party of Korea),
   162–63
Bush, George H.W., 107

camps, work/prison, 39–47, 65, 96,
   204, 223, 236; and knowledge
   of Kim Jong-nam, 41–43, 49;
   punishments/atrocities at, 46, 243;
   Shin's internment at, 51, 179, 185,
   221, 227; survivors' accounts of,
   41–46; U.S. mapping of, 40
Cao de Benós de Les y Pérez,
   Alejandro, 186–88
Catherine the Great, German
   television movie about, 91–92
Central Intelligence Agency (CIA),
   8, 129, 158, 204
Charles V (Holy Roman Emperor),
   104

MAGNUS BÄRTÅS is an artist and professor of fine arts at Konstfack, the University College of Arts, Crafts and Design in Stockholm. Among other works, he has published an anthology about the borderland between literature and the visual arts.

FREDRIK EKMAN is a writer, librettist, and editor based in Stockholm. His musical works have toured across Europe.

MAGNUS BÄRTÅS and FREDRIK EKMAN have written three books together.

SASKIA VOGEL is a writer and a translator from Swedish. Her translations include *The Summer of Kim Novak* by Håkan Nesser and *Who Cooked Adam Smith's Dinner?* by Katrine Marçal. She is also the Swedish series editor and translator for Readux Books. She lives in Berlin.

CPSIA information can be obtained at www.ICGtesting.com
Printed in the USA
LVOW12s0014020316

477281LV00008B/31/P